FREEDOM TO BE HAPPY

The Business Case for Happiness

Matt Phelan

Happiness and Humans Publishing

H&H

Cover design by: Joe Wedgwood

CONTENTS

Happiness

PREFACE. LEARNING TO READ...

Hey everyone, my name is Matt.

Like you, I want to be happy, and also probably like you, because you picked up this book on happiness or maybe you just liked the pink and yellow cover that Joe designed for me (cheers, Joe), I suspect you also have an interest in happiness in the workplace.

Before we jump into the book, I thought I should introduce myself.

I was born in the spring of 1982 in a small port and seaside town called Harwich in Essex which, for the geographers out there, is in the South East of England about 60 miles from the capital London. I spent the first 18 years of my life growing up on a farm with my parents, two older sisters, and two younger brothers. You can probably already sense the middle child syndrome leaping out of the pages at you.

I don't want to bore you with my childhood, but there are two significant things that fascinated me about growing up on a farm immersed in nature. Despite animals having less sophisticated communication skills than human beings, they seem in my opinion often better equipped to communicate how they feel.

When I was really young, I was enthralled by how my dad could read how animals were feeling: if they were ill, if they needed feeding or if they required medical attention even though they couldn't talk. Anyone reading this with a cat or dog will know what I am talking about.

Growing up with an Irish mum in a very English town also fascinated me. The English are world champions at not discussing their emotions, but my mum could always sense how people were feeling without them saying. I have never met someone so loved and ready to share a hug to cheer someone up or to just simply sit and listen.

I carried this awe for how my dad could read animals and my mum could read humans from a non-verbal perspective into my career. I love people watching; I could spend hours peering out of a coffee shop window just watching the world go by.

I hated school with a passion and constantly felt I was in a daytime jail I couldn't escape. It wasn't until I was playing with friends or I returned to the countryside that I felt free and happy. I met some amazing friends at school and still hang out with many of them to this day. I scraped by in my exams and made it to Canterbury University in Kent. At Canterbury I studied Marketing and Geography (weird combination, I know). Canterbury was also the city where I met my co-founders of The Happiness Index, Chris Hyland and Tony Latter (more on those two punks later).

I enjoyed university much more than school, in part because I felt I was there of my own free will. After travelling the world with Tony in 2003, I started a marketing career working for a startup in the education sector (thanks for taking a chance on me, Denise) and then moved to London to work for a research and events company that was eventually acquired by the Guardian Media Group.

After leaving the Guardian, I got my dream job at a media company working on the Barclays, KFC and Marks & Spencer accounts. In month one I realised my dream job was not my dream job. I did not like the culture of where I worked, and I did not feel like I belonged. I left after three months (such a snowflake) and started a digital and data company called 4Ps Marketing in 2008 with Chris Hyland. We had hopes and dreams of creating a global marketing agency with a thriving culture but first of all we just wanted to have fun. Four months into that venture, the 2008 financial crisis hit. We rode that out, and eight years later we successfully sold that business.

Following a four-month sabbatical in that beautifully hot summer where the England footy team got to the semi-finals of the World Cup (i.e. summer 2018), we decided to invest our remaining proceeds from the sale of our marketing agency into a business we had started four years earlier called The Happiness Index.

I have written this book as despite the now overwhelming evidence that workplaces with happier staff perform financially better, there is still an entrenched view that emotions like happiness belong at home and only so-called serious business discussions belong in the boardroom.

Thank you for picking up this book, and, if you do read it all, please message me with your honest feedback. I want to hear from you, and I want to hear about your journey with happiness.

I hope you enjoy.

Matt

Dedication

I captured this photo of my children on our morning walk in Spring 2020 in the park near our home in North London. At the time of the photo we were in lockdown due to the Covid-19 pandemic and we were only permitted to leave the house once a day. These daily walks together as a family are the happiest memories I have from my entire life. I dedicate this book to my children Izzy and Fred for making me laugh (and often cry) every single day.

CHAPTER 1. WHY HAPPINESS?

Background

For the last 12 years I have been making notes on my entrepreneurial journey and for the last six years we have been collecting millions of data points on happiness in the workplace. In 2020, like many of you, I found myself being locked down due to the Covid-19 pandemic.

This pandemic has caused havoc and impacted us all in many negative ways. However, it has also presented us with a unique opportunity to slow down and evaluate life. I wrote this book to make sense of the past but also to share ideas on how I think we can create a better world for the future.

This book took six months to write, but it has been 12 years in the making. Covid-19 has been a wake-up call that the way we have been living and working isn't sustainable or healthy. It certainly wasn't working for me.

Making sense of the world

Humans love taking things apart to understand how they work. It's human nature and it's how we make sense of the world. By breaking things down we have made many advances as a species in everything from medicine to flight. The benefits of breaking things down are clear, but the downside of breaking things down is that we may just lose the magic that is created by the sum of the parts.

The heart and brain divide

The Industrial Revolution moved workers from the countryside to urban areas in record numbers. This revolution led to huge advancements and in the process of breaking things down to machine level detail we lost something. We divided the heart and the brain in the pursuit of profits. Today we are seeing record levels of burnout, lowering levels of productivity, mental health is at breaking point, and companies are struggling to attract and retain talent.

On a weekly basis I get calls from CEOs and HR directors across the globe that I have never met or worked with, but they call me because they are confused as to why their employee engagement scores are at a record high but their people are unhappy and leaving the business. They want to understand why.

The command and control systems used today to run companies are relics of the factory floor and are killing modern organisations. This death is not going to be a quick one but a much more painful death more akin to a slow burning cancer. Employee engagement is broken, and human emotions have been banned from the workplace.

The outcome

We have banned emotions in the workplace, and we label them unprofessional. Emotions belong at home and rational thinking belongs at work in this crazy world we have created. We have broken what it is to be human, and, even worse, we reward and reinforce employees that leave their emotions at home.

We chase these rewards in schools, workplaces, and life in the hope that this success will eventually pay the bills and make us happy.

Flip the script

However, researchers, philosophers, and practitioners across the globe have started to question the wisdom that success leads to happiness and argue that in actual fact happiness leads to success. The happiness trio Sonja Lyubomirsky, Ed Diener, and Laura King pointed this out in their 2005 paper, "The Benefits of Frequent Positive Affect: Does Happiness Lead to Success?":

> We have reviewed extensive evidence demonstrating that happy people are successful and flourishing people. Part of the explanation for this phenomenon undoubtedly comes from the fact that success leads to happiness. Our review, however, focuses on the reverse causal direction – that happiness, in turn, leads to success. Happy people show more frequent positive affect and specific adaptive characteristics. Positive affect has been shown, in experimental, longitudinal, and correlational studies, to lead to these specific adaptive characteristics. Thus, the evidence seems to support our conceptual model that happiness causes many of the successful outcomes with which it correlates.

Since this 2005 paper more and more research backs up this shift in thinking, but we now need to move the story forward to the modern day.

The story
The goal of this book is to reconnect the heart and brain within organisations. I want to help people see emotions such as happiness as data points that are equally as important as say revenue or productivity. I want to show you how these data points should not compete but that they are all part of the same interrelated ecosystem.

The cast
To tell this story, you will hear from philosophers with new ideas, researchers with data, and practitioners with front line experience.

The Happiness and Humans Community and podcast
To make this book a living beast, I have created a podcast and

community so that you can listen to people in this book discuss their POV in more detail and meet like-minded people on similar journeys to create a more positive world of work.

Community
You can join The Happiness and Humans Community here: tinyurl.com/joinhappyhumans

Podcast
You can listen to the *Happiness and Humans* podcast here: tinyurl.com/HappinessAndHumans

The business case for happiness
This book aims to give you the tools to make your business case for happiness. The best thing about all the advice, data, and research in this book is that it is all free to implement. You just need a well-researched business case to get you over the line.

CHAPTER 2. WHAT IS HAPPINESS?

What is happiness to me?

For me, happiness is independence within all my relationships from work, to friends, to family. I am a sociable guy, but I also need to feel free within all my relationships to be happy. This feeling of freedom is what allows me to perform at work and be happy in life. It's probably what drove me to be an entrepreneur and also what drives me to help companies create cultures where employees can be themselves and thrive.

For me, happiness is freedom.

Before we make a business case for happiness, we need to define what happiness actually is. Of all the questions in this book, this is the hardest to answer…

So, let's pretend to be Bill and Ted and go WAY back in time.

Before we can explore how happiness can drive performance, it is important to take a look back at some of the happiness influencers who have informed how we think about happiness to this day.

According to genetic and fossil evidence, older versions of Homo sapiens evolved in Africa between 200,000 and 100,000 years ago. The fact that we all originate from the same common ancestors in Africa is all the evidence you need to confirm that being a racist makes you a complete plonker (sorry, not sorry). Members of one branch left Africa around 90,000 years ago. Over time, they replaced earlier human populations such as Neanderthals and Homo erectus. Our hunter-gatherer forebearers formed families and social groups, put down roots, and picked up tools (basically early forms of the iPad). And so, slowly, we turned into agricultural superstars, freeing up our enormous brains to accumulate what humans will – wealth and power. But this starts to open up the question: were we happy and what is happiness?

Of course, with no written record, it's hard to tell whether our ancestors were happy. We simply don't know. Agriculture was backbreaking work, archaeologists suggest that their diet was less nutritious and satisfying than the hunter-gatherers that went before them, and diseases were rampant. However, we can't ask them how they were feeling about any of this.

If this is the case, let's fast forward to a time when we do have a record of happiness.

Confucius

And so, we find ourselves in 551 BC, in the Lu Province in China. The province is relatively small, but, sitting as it does on the wide fertile banks of the Yellow River, it has gained prosperity and power. We are going to treat this area as the birthplace of the history of happiness.

We've come here to meet Confucius, one of the world's best-known philosophers. He was born in 551 BC, the son of a low-level official who died when he was young and so was brought up by a single mother. But he grew up to become a powerful politician who founded a philosophical movement that still shapes the way we see the world today.

The trouble with writing about Confucius is that the internet loves to attribute quotes to him with no good sources to suggest that he actually said them. Here's one of my favourites:

"You cannot buy happiness, but you have to pay the price."

Importantly for our history of happiness, we do have evidence that Confucius described himself as a happy man. When one of his students struggled to describe him, he came up with the following suggestion:

"He is the sort of man who forgets to eat when he engages

himself in vigorous pursuit of learning, who is so full of joy that he forgets his worries, and who does not notice that old age is coming on."

Confucius suggested that being a good person would make you a happy person. He helpfully distilled this into five core principles, which are known as the Five Constants. They are:

- *Ren* or humanity or altruism;
- *Li* or living by social or religious norms;
- *Yi* or righteousness or living by your morals;
- *Zhi* the love of learning; and, finally;
- *Xin* or the act of being true to yourself and living with integrity.

You'll notice that there's a common thread amongst these things, namely an interactivity: living well isn't worth doing if you're not with other people. Whether you're serving others (*Ren*), learning with or from others (*Zhi*), or showing others your true self (*Xin*), there's an interrelatedness to the Confucian understanding of happiness. Fundamentally, Confucius states we can be human, and therefore happy, within the wider group.

Aristotle

Our journey through the history of happiness takes us next to 3rd century BC Athens, the cradle of philosophical thought. Despite the somewhat warlike reputation of Athens (not helped by Hollywood's depictions or indeed by Greek mythology), during this period we see a proliferation of the bigger names in Western philosophical thought. We've come, though, to visit Aristotle.

Aristotle, who had been born outside the city, came to Athens as a teenager to study. By the time he left, aged 34, he'd furnished the city with a philosophy school at the Lyceum, which housed a library of his books on papyrus scrolls. Within these works he had a lot to say about happiness, one of the most succinct is this affirmation: "Happiness depends on ourselves."

Having been taught philosophy by Plato, it's perhaps no surprise that Aristotle made it into the big leagues of the pioneers of happiness. His main contribution, as I see it, is that he introduced the idea of *eudaimonia*.

Aristotle said that: "*Eudaimonia* is the meaning and the purpose of life, the whole aim and end of human existence."

Simply put, Aristotle believed that the only purpose of humans as a species is this elusive *eudaimonia*. Even if your ancient Greek isn't very sharp, I think you'll probably have realised by now that this concept can be translated as wellbeing or perhaps happiness.

Stoics

Having visited Aristotle, let's make our way to the north side of the Angora to the Stoa Poikile. This 'Painted Porch' was hung with paintings of the bloody battles that the city state of Athens had won and decorated with the loot of war. Here, below the Ionic columns, we meet Zeno and his followers who are founding the Stoic movement, named after the building where it was created.

As a father of two children, I know I am not allowed to have a favourite child, but I must admit that the Stoics are my favourite happiness pioneers. I take a lot personally from the Stoics, but unfortunately little writing from these early Stoics survives, and so our journey follows the influence of their work on Roman thinkers.

Roman Stoics built on the ideas of Aristotle, expounding something very similar to *eudaimonia*, but, like Confucius, they had a small number of elements on which they founded their ideas of happiness.

Perhaps the best summary of the Stoic approach to happiness comes from Epictetus in his short work, *The Handbook*. He stresses the importance of focusing on what we can control and accepting that we can't control much of what we experience.

"There is only one way to happiness and that is to cease worrying about things which are beyond the power or our will."

This simple statement has definitely helped me as entrepreneur working through times like the 2008 financial crash and the 2020 global pandemic.

Epictetus builds on this to say that we can control how we respond to events. And finally, he encourages people to be their best selves: to focus on the present and to be the best they can be today.

How can we be the best people we can be? This seems much easier said than done. Stoics believe that virtue is derived from reason and self-control. This is perhaps where Stoics get their slightly dour reputation from. Stoics believe they should live according to the virtues of wisdom, bravery, and justice; it's a shame modern society has fixated on their appreciation of moderation.

Perhaps the easiest way of thinking about living by these virtues in the modern world is to think about becoming a part of something larger than yourself. Take your strengths, skills, and sense of justice, and channel these principles into creating a life, a job, and a system of beliefs which you can fully embody. The Stoics suggest that by doing this you can become truly happy.

Freud

Our journey through the history of happiness now takes a giant leap forward to 1856 because we're here to visit Sigmund Freud.

Freud is Austrian born, studying and qualifying as a doctor, and setting up his practice in Vienna. As the father of psychotherapy, it's no surprise that Freud had a lot to say about happiness. Like Aristotle and the Stoics before him, Freud believed that fundamentally humans strive to be happy. However, he made the additional assertion that we are all trying to avoid the negative, while we simultaneously try to embrace the positive.

> [People] strive after happiness; they want to become happy and to remain so. This endeavour has two sides, a positive and a negative aim. It aims, on the one hand, at an absence of pain and displeasure, and, on the other, at the experiencing of strong feelings of pleasure.

Unfortunately, sometimes, in trying to avoid pain and suffering, Freud suggests we inadvertently miss out on some of the best bits in life. For example, Freud thinks work and a career is a great path to happiness:

> *No other technique for the conduct of life attaches the individual so firmly to reality as laying emphasis on work; for his work at least gives him a secure place in a portion of reality, in the human community. And yet, as a path to happiness, work is not highly prized by men. They do not strive after it as they do after other possibilities of satisfaction.*

Interestingly, in Chapter 13: The Happiness Index Data, we will see that there is a lot of truth in what Freud describes here. In this chapter, we will show how an employee having an opportunity to progress is really important to their happiness.

During his long and productive career, Freud wrote 23 books (luckily for you, I can't see myself writing that many books) and countless papers, so we can't cover his whole oeuvre and how it relates to happiness, but there is one other thread that it would be useful to pull out here. Freud believed that there was no truer happiness than when feelings are reciprocated. These might be, and, according to Freud, often are, romantic feelings, but there is also happiness to be found in the reciprocation of friendship, trust, and loyalty. Once again, we will see the importance of relationships pop back up in our data chapter.

Positive psychology

Our journey now takes us to present day America. With all the benefits modern life brings us, from technology to creature comforts, you'd think that we'd find ourselves in the happiest moment of all. However, as you probably already know, particularly since you're reading a book about happiness, it doesn't always quite work out this way.

We've come to New York to meet Martin Seligman, a pioneer of positive psychology. Seligman studied at Princeton, Oxford and the University of Pennsylvania, where he now is a professor of psychology. He writes self-help books and gives Ted Talks and is one of the most pre-eminent voices in the theories of happiness around today.

Building on the work of Abraham Maslow, who first coined the term in 1954, Seligman founded the study of positive psychology in 1998 as a reaction to what he saw as the focus on the negative and the disordered in the field of psychology.

Seligman says: "The skills of becoming happy turn out to be almost entirely different from the skills of not being sad, not being anxious, or not being angry."

Seligman suggests there are three kinds of happiness, each of which is experienced in different ways and at different times.

The first kind of happiness is flow. This is the *eudaimonia* that Aristotle spoke of and the joy Confucius found in being completely absorbed in learning. Flow is the kind of happiness you feel when you're really enjoying your work and find yourself carried along in the current of your tasks.

The second kind of happiness is meaning. This is the kind of happiness the Stoics talked about – building a life that takes your skills and beliefs and allows you to channel them.

The final kind of happiness Seligman describes is pleasure. This is the kind of happiness that Freud discussed: the happiness that comes from experiences and people in the moment.

Since Seligman founded positive psychology, there have been many notable names who have added their voices to the growing swell of published research, philosophical debate, and self-help books. These include happiness pioneers like Carol Dweck, Barbara Fredrickson, Ed Diener, and Christopher Peterson.

So, there we have it, a whistle-stop tour of how humans have attempted to define happiness through the ages.

The more I learn about happiness, the harder I find it to define happiness. BUT, as I've also learned, this doesn't actually matter so much. I will explain as we go.

CHAPTER 3. CAN MONEY MAKE YOU HAPPY?

Many of us genuinely believe that having more money will make us happier, and others feel equally sure that money can't buy happiness. So, who is right? Although many philosophers, economists, and psychologists have asked this question over the generations, there's still not one conclusive answer. As ever with happiness (and a lot of life's more thorny and interesting questions), the answer seems to be, it depends.

Let's take a deeper dive into the things that complicate the relationship between happiness and money, looking first at simply the act of having or earning money, before thinking about how we choose to spend it.

Can having money make me happy?

The simple answer to this question is yes. Having money can make you happy. However, only up to a point, and that happiness also depends on how you came by your money.

How happy does my salary make me?

Many studies have looked at how much effect your salary has on your happiness. Of course, your salary might affect a bunch of other elements, such as the size of your home, the way you decorate it, and perhaps the area you live in.

As the wellbeing expert Gethin Nadin says: "Money contributes to happiness when it helps us make basic needs, but the research tells us that above a certain level more money doesn't actually yield more happiness."

Sonja Lyubomirsky, a psychology professor at the University

of California, wanted to find out if she could find the salary that was needed for happiness. She asked people making $30,000 per annum how much they thought they'd need to be happy. The answer? Fifty thousand dollars. When she asked people making $100,000 per year, they estimated they'd need $250,000. Ultimately, her study showed that no matter how much individuals earned, they always thought they needed a little more to be truly happy.

An often cited 2010 study out of Princeton suggested that happiness is linked to salary, but only to a point. Happiness seemed to increase with salary up to a value of $75,000 per annum. After this amount, there seemed to be less correlation between increased salaries and increased happiness. The study also showed that increased salaries (to the point of $75k per annum), also decreased the impact of negative circumstances on happiness. For example, those who earned more were less likely to feel sad even if they were going through a divorce or were suffering from severe asthma.

Of course, how happy your money makes you is also linked to what you do with it (more on that later), so there's a little more to the story than you might think.

The case of millionaires and inherited money

An interesting exception to the previously discussed limit on the happiness produced by income is the case of millionaires. It seems that, although the 2010 study discussed above replicated findings from earlier studies, there was something missing in their data.

First of all, most studies linking the effects of wealth and happiness only account for income, rather than net-worth, which excludes money which has been inherited or otherwise is part of a person's total financial situation. Secondly, many studies looked at those who fall within 'average' wage earner boundaries. In short, millionaires were underrepresented in the data.

A 2017 study found that there was a significant difference in happiness between those worth between $1–3 million, compared to those with fortunes of $10 million and above. It seems that decamillionaires are actually statistically happier than their poor multimillionaire cousins. However, the study also showed that those who had earned their own way into their lifestyle were far happier than those who had been born into the lap of luxury.

In short, it seems that Andrew Carnegie was right when he famously said that leaving your children "enormous wealth generally deadens the talents and energies of the child, leading to a less useful and less worthy life than they otherwise would".

The lottery effect

A final interesting area of study amongst happiness researchers is the case of those who have won money. There are many studies into this, as it gives a great indication of money in isolation of other confounding variables, such as socio-economic class, geographical location, and so on. This is because there are plenty of people (all those who did not win the lottery) who can be used as controls for these variables in the wider population.

Generally, the science seems to suggest that happiness isn't particularly increased for those who have won moderate or even large sums of money. A study in 1978 looking at 22 lottery winners, with average takings of $480,000, showed that there was no significant difference in how happy winners were compared to control groups. In fact, those who had had pay-outs reported that ordinary activities, such as watching television or socialising with friends, brought them less happiness than those who hadn't won. Interestingly, a later study in 2007 found that those who won around $200,000 experienced greater mental stress in the year that they won but were likely to be happier two years after their windfall.

In a 2018 literature review, Grant E. Donnelly et al. came to the conclusion that moderately sized lottery winnings may increase happiness, but only slightly. In short, as with the millionaires example, it's not just how much money you have, but what determines how happy money makes you is how you got it.

Can spending money make me happy?

Of course, it's not all about having money. The ways in which we spend the money we have also has a significant impact on how happy we think we're going to be. The saying goes that money can't buy happiness, but is this true?

Spending money on experiences

One of the best-known pieces of happiness research in recent times is a widely reported study in 2014 by Thomas Gilovich. His study showed that spending money on experiences makes people happier than spending money on things.

From his research, Gilovich was able to draw several conclusions as to why this might be. Firstly, experiential purchases are more likely to increase your social ties. This might be because you're more likely to share the experience with someone else, or because you're more likely to talk about it with others afterward.

Also, your experiences are more likely to form part of your identity than your possessions; for example, you might be the kind of person who regularly goes to the football with a season ticket, or you may prefer to go on cruises with your pals. And lastly, you're less likely to compare your experiences to those of other people. Your holiday in the south of France was fab, but it's much harder to say if it's better or worse than your colleague's holiday to Cornwall, than it is to directly compare your cars, for example.

This research often gets used to suggest that money can buy you happiness as long as you spend it in the right way. Certainly, Gilovich's conclusions seem to bear out this point. However, can you spend money in other areas and still buy a little happiness?

Spending money on things

Perceived wisdom suggests that buying things won't make you happy, and although this is something many of us know, it's still a thought pattern we may slip into. Who hasn't been caught in a loop of thinking that a faster computer, a new games console, or your favourite team's latest football shirt won't make you even a little happier in the moment?

The problem is, of course, that this happiness is just that – in the moment. Because of the hedonic adaptation discussed in the previous chapter, our brains simply get used to the stuff around us. This means that we're less likely to get sustained happiness from the things we've spent our money on as time goes on.

However, there are things we can do to increase the happiness we gain from buying things.

A 2011 study by Elizabeth Dunn and her team at the University of British Columbia suggested that should you wish to buy material possessions, then you should think about buying several smaller treats, spend time thinking about your purchases, and consider the benefits that the purchase has on your day-to-day life more generally.

Spending money on other people

Another factor to consider is that buying things for other people makes us considerably happier than buying things for ourselves.

Elizabeth Dunn has done further studies on what she calls "prosocial" spending, or spending money on others. When asked, most people think that when given a small amount of money, they would prefer to spend it on themselves than on others. However, Dunn's research shows that spending even small amounts on other people can increase happiness by far more than spending that money on yourself would do.

I personally understand this feeling. I actually don't like receiving presents myself, but I do really enjoy giving them. No matter how much you explain this to friends or family, it is always going to come off as ungrateful. Most presents I receive I give to charity.

In her study, Dunn gave money to participants who were randomly assigned into one of two groups. One had to spend that money on someone else and the other on themselves. Dunn found that the group that spent the $5 on someone else not only gained a larger bump in happiness, but that it also lasted for longer. This seems to be because spending money on others is a social activity and so helps us with social bonding, as well as giving us a better opinion of ourselves (even when the gifting was forced by scientists!). It's important to note that Dunn only gave her participants $5, so it's not even like you need to be spending a lot of money at a time to make yourself and those around you happier.

Spending money on time

The only thing I really splash out money on is buying time. I have been known to calculate my journey home to see my kids and workout how I can buy more time with my kids. I have changed planes, trains, and automobiles to spend more time with my children. I remember paying an extra £20 for a taxi home that bought me an extra 10 minutes with my children before they went to bed. Two quid per minute with my kids seemed cheap to me.

The good news for me is the data shows spending money on time makes us happier, and that is to, quite literally, buy ourselves more time. There are a number of ways we can buy time. Firstly, we can work less because we can afford to. We can also pay others to do work we don't enjoy, such as cleaning, ironing, or doing our accounts. Alternatively, we can invest in equipment or tools that make such jobs easier, such as a dishwasher or a robotic vacuum cleaner.

According to Lyubomirsky, if this time gets reinvested into activities which empirical and anecdotal evidence suggests bring happiness, then this can bring a lot of joy into your life. These kinds of activities include spending time with friends or family, enjoying music, film or other cultural events, learning a new skill, or volunteering your time to charity.

Again, on a work level, there isn't much that annoys me more than an employee not reporting a slow laptop. Can there be a bigger waste of money than paying out a wage for an employee and then giving them a laptop that takes 15 minutes to load?

Worry

A 2020 study showed that worrying about money was a bigger cause of stress for individuals than concerns about work and even relationships. This level of stress means that money worries are impacting people's work. In fact, on average, each employee loses about 1.5 to three days a year to stress about money, so over the whole workforce this can really add up. When it comes to filtering happiness down the company, it makes sense then to start by ensuring that your company is doing everything it can be to alleviate this stress.

Gethin Nadin believes that as money worries affect work, this means that employers should become involved in the financial lives of their employees. Studies have found that trust in financial services is at an all-time low in the Western world; indeed, it's lower than any other industry. However, people have a very high level of trust in their own employer. As it happens, in recent years, an individual's employer has consistently ranked as the most trusted institution in a person's life.

Nadin argues that this trust is fostered as employers invest in people's wellbeing more generally. He states that this means that employers are in a unique situation whereby they can help with the financial, and therefore ultimately the mental wellbeing of their employees.

As we've seen, this means that employers are not simply looking after their people and doing the morally right thing – taking care of an employee's financial and emotional wellbeing may also impact their absenteeism, an idea we will return to in a later chapter.

So yeah, money can make you happy in some ways, but be careful what you wish for...

CHAPTER 4. IS HAPPINESS NATURE OR NURTURE?

When growing up, your parents and siblings – if you are fortunate to have either – will have a big impact on your happiness.

When considering what causes some people to be happy, while others are not, and the degrees of happiness which separate the two, there are various factors which come into play. Here, the 'nature versus nurture' debate comes into play. Are some people just born happy? Are we able to impact our own happiness at all? Or do some people simply have the secret to happiness?

Well, as ever with these situations, the truth of the situation is that there isn't one absolute source of truth, and nature and nurture both come into play. Remember that bit in *Star Wars* about only Sith Lords deal in absolutes? That is certainly the case here.

John Lennon felt that nurture came into play, when he is reported to have said:

"When I was five years old, my mother always told me that happiness was the key to life. When I went to school, they asked me what I wanted to be when I grew up. I wrote down 'happy'. They told me I didn't understand the assignment, and I told them they didn't understand life."

This would suggest that Lennon believed that happiness is something you work towards – that it is something that you can achieve. Let's turn to science to see if this is true. Can anyone become happy? Or are some people hampered by their genes?

Before we start, it's important to take into account that the science here leaves significant margin for error. The figures are probably going to vary between individuals and maybe even across the course of your life. Furthermore, different studies have come to slightly varying conclusions. For the purposes of this book, I have decided to work with the numbers that prominent happiness scientist Sonja Lyubomirsky found following her extensive testing.

Lyubomirsky suggests that around 50% of your happiness is genetic; that is to say that half of your happiness is decided by your nature. The remaining 50% of your happiness makeup is divided between two areas – we'll call them 'environment' and 'the way you think'. Your environment makes up 10% of your happiness, and the way you think makes up the remaining 40%.

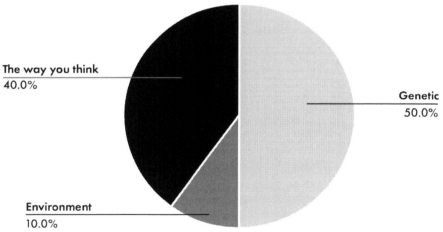

Figure 1: What Makes Up Happiness?

In order to come to these answers, Lyubomirsky conducted a study looking at the happiness of over 2,000 twins. This meant that the study was able to ascertain what percentage of happiness is determined by genetics compared to other elements.

The real message I want you to take away from this chapter is that both nature and nurture play a part in our happiness. It might be useful at this stage to take the time to define what we mean exactly by each of these three elements.

The first 50%: genetics

We've already talked about the fact that some people are 'naturally' happier than others. Those of you who have children may have seen this in action – although your children are likely to have pretty similar upbringing and environments, you may find that one just seems to be happier than their siblings. Similarly, when you think back to people you knew when you were a child, there were probably kids you remember being happy, outgoing, and positive. It's likely that these people are still exhibiting these personality traits. Meanwhile, those who were more serious, pessimistic, or negative are potentially also still that way.

A happiness gene?

There isn't a specific gene which controls happiness. To date, scientists have identified over 300 genomes which are related to one's natural proclivity towards happiness. Genetic scientists think the genetic elements they've studied so far probably make up around 2% of neurological differences – so this is an area of research which is going to keep some very smart people very busy for a long time to come.

The happiness 'set point'

Science suggests we have what is sometimes called a genetic 'set point' for happiness. This means that regardless of our environment and the way we think, there's a certain level of happiness which we are always going to return to over time. You may be more familiar with the weight set point which is the concept that there's a certain weight your body 'thinks' it needs to be to stand the best chance of survival, and it will always try to return to that weight. Well, a similar concept looks likely in happiness. Your mind has certain genes and will release certain hormones to keep you a specific level of happiness.

Scientists did several tests to confirm that this happiness set point is genetic and stable over time. They tested sets of identical and fraternal twins' happiness at age 20 and age 30. They found that identical twins had similar levels of happiness compared to fraternal twins. They also found that the happiness that the twins felt at age 20 was within the same range as the happiness they felt at age 30. In short, this set point is genetic and changes little over time.

Is our happiness linked to our nature?

Essentially, the scientific evidence shows that around half of our happiness comes down to our genetics. Or, to put it another way, our nature. But don't get too disillusioned just yet; we still have another 50% to play with.

What about the remaining 50%? Let's look into that in more detail...

The 10%: environment

Your environment is the portion of happiness which people put the most stock in. Who hasn't thought that they'll be happier when they have a slightly bigger home, a car that's a model newer than their current one, or a higher job title? We all naturally feel that having nice things, like a high-flying job and a beautiful home, is going to make or break our happiness. But actually, the science suggests that these things have less of an effect than you might think.

What do you mean by environment?

What we're talking about here are your circumstances. This could include your job, home, or car. It could also include whether you're married with kids or are happily living a single lifestyle. Other factors that fall into this category might include whether you've recently won the lottery or whether you've come into money. What we're looking at here are the creature comforts we build up around ourselves or our 'stuff'– essentially anything which affects your physical environment.

Assuming you live a relatively affluent life, with access to food, a safe home, and a comfortable place to sleep, your environment makes up as little as 10% of your total happiness.

Why is this?

The stuff around us has a limited impact on our happiness because our brains are hardwired to get used to good things. In the scientific community, this is called hedonic adaptation. As humans, we very quickly become used to the nice things in our lives – the pay rises, the cars, the new house – and all these things just become background noise. We always want slightly bigger homes, slightly newer cars, slightly better phones, and so on.

But you might be saying to yourself, "I'm not as materialistic as you, mate, all I need to be happy is to get married to the person of my dreams and we'll live happily ever after", I've got bad news for you too. The human brain's ability to get used to things even extends to wedded bliss. In fact, studies have found that the increase in happiness brought on from being married only lasts for two years.

The final 40%: the way we think

Really this is the exciting bit, the bit we actually have control over and can harness to improve our happiness. Not only can we help make ourselves happy, but also those around us.

Going back to the quote from earlier, we can see that according to this story John Lennon's mum had the right idea about happiness – that it's something to be worked towards – and this is a way of thinking she passed on to her son. Now whether John Lennon was able to achieve that happiness which the legend has it he sought early on in life is another question, but he started out looking in the right direction.

The realm of positive psychologists

This 40% of happiness has been studied a lot by some of the happiness pioneers mentioned in the positive psychologists section in Chapter 2. Positive psychologists are interested in learning more about the ways in which people who are particularly psychologically well are able to feel happy. For this reason, rather than studying people with mental illness, they focus on those who are particularly happy. By doing this, scientists have been able to isolate behaviours which happy people have and are likely to correlate with increased happiness. They then have healthy people, or those with depression or low mood, complete these behaviours to see if they're likely to help everyone be happier.

Through this kind of study scientists have found that, as the Stoics suggested, certain ways of thinking are likely to help people be happier. Essentially, what we see from the scientific studies conducted by positive psychologists is that the way we think about the stuff that surrounds us has a much higher effect on happiness than the actual stuff itself. This is particularly evident when we look at studies around gratitude and savouring.

So, is happiness a solo endeavour?

Importantly, the behaviours studied by positive psychologists aren't necessarily ways of thinking that need to be done on your own. In particular, feeling close or connected to your community, be that where you live or work, is related to positive happiness outcomes.

Similarly, feeling and expressing emotions such as gratitude and taking the time to savour moments of joy are all behaviours which are seen in those who are particularly happy. Research has shown that those of us who aren't naturally happy can improve our overall feelings of wellbeing by replicating these behaviours.

Practicing things like forgiveness and gratitude, as well as savouring moments of joy, are all ways of thinking which not only can make you happier, but which can also make those around you happier. In fact, studies have shown that sharing positive emotions makes you feel better than simply noting the positive emotions on your own. Furthermore, letting other people know about these positive emotions is likely to make them feel better too.

These kinds of behaviours are more important in the workplace than you might think. Studies show that just the act of sincerely and honestly showing gratitude for someone's efforts, particularly in private, can have a profound positive effect on their happiness. Similarly, having strong bonds and relationships is a key factor in happiness, and this is also something that you can work on in the workplace, ensuring that you take the time to get to know and interact with your team and wider colleagues.

CHAPTER 5. IS HAPPINESS A FLUFFY METRIC?

So we can blow this fluffy thing out of the water in the first few chapters and you can put this book down and head to the pub, I will offer up the most shocking study on employee engagement of which I am aware.

In 2012, Michael West and Jeremy Dawson published a paper with the King's Fund that still shocks me. Their research looked into the link between employee engagement and job performance. The study reviewed existing literature and evidence alongside NHS employee surveys and a range of job performance metrics including absenteeism and turnover, patient satisfaction, and mortality, as well as safety measures.

The study found a number of clear associations between employee engagement and job performance. We might intuitively feel that patients would do better when being seen by happy medical staff, but this study showed the association conclusively, backing up instinct with data. Strikingly, the data showed that an 'ordinary' increase in overall employee engagement, could lead to a 2.4% decrease in mortality rates. That is HUGE.

The study also found clear areas which are associated to employee engagement. These results aren't just applicable for the NHS and the health sector but are equally relevant to the wider world of work. In particular appraisals, team structure and job design are highlighted. The report concludes by stating "when we care for staff, they can fulfil their calling of providing outstanding professional care for patients".

I spoke to Jeremy Dawson recently and he also uncovered some even more worrying data related to discrimination and equality in the workplace. Jump onto my *Happiness and Humans* podcast interview with him if you want to find out more.

So, in summary, if there were two hospitals where everything was the same and one had happy staff and one had unhappy staff, the one with the unhappy staff is more likely to have a higher mortality rate. The study also goes on to make an association between employee engagement and infection rates which is a hugely relevant point at the moment.

So perhaps we should finish the book here?! Unhappiness is killing people... Why do we need to go any further?

But we can't stop here. This paper was published in 2012 and most people have never heard of it. The hard-nosed business professionals who only dream of profit will point out they don't run a hospital and will cry, "We are a business, not a charity".

This paper on its own should be enough to build a case for happy employees, but we are going to need more data, more stories, and more case studies (shocking, I know – no pub for you just yet).

So many questions...

Think back to a time when you were happy... Can you see it? Can you smell it? Can you taste it? Can you hear it? Can you touch it?

When I think back I can taste ice cream on Walton Pier, I can still see the sun setting over Café del Mar by the sea in Ibiza with my school friends, the musty old smell of Canterbury cathedral when I graduated, the sound of my children playing in the garden, and the zenith of my happy memories is my wife and I holding both our children in our arms after they were born.

However...

The opposite is also true.

I can remember feeling the pain as a bald-headed rugby forward ran straight into my head in 2004 and concussed me; I can still physically feel that to this day on the top right of my head. I remember watching the news as the 2008 financial crisis unfolded just as I had started my first business, hearing my dad telling me over the phone how much the foot and mouth crisis was crippling our farm, and I definitely remember being forced to eat brussels sprouts for the first time by my grandma. YUCK!

I also don't think that unhappy people can't perform. And, in many cases, unhappiness can be a driver to start, to change your life for the better. I started my first business as I was unhappy with the culture of the place I was working.

A business case for happiness

So, the NHS study clearly shows that happiness isn't fluffy, but to prove happiness is a serious business metric, we are going to need to show how long-term sustainable happiness can drive an organisation forward. We are going to need to see this translate into cold, hard profit and loss.

To help make a business case, I will need the superstar of shapes to help me. The humble triangle with its incredibly strong angles will be the physical form of my argument.

Here are my three angles:

1) The philosophers / the storytellers
2) The practitioners / front line case studies
3) The evidence / data science and insight

Building a business case is difficult, but the best ones I have seen are a good mix of data, evidence, and a bit of magic sprinkled on by a good storyteller.

All humans think differently, and I want to combine the art of storytelling that the philosophers bring, present live examples from the current front line of business and underpin everything with cold hard data and evidence.

I'm an entrepreneur, I'm not a philosopher, a scientist, or a practitioner, so I am excited to introduce you to these experts to help make our business case for happiness together. I believe and have seen first-hand that happiness can drive a business, and I want to use this book to inspire you to do the same.

But before I introduce them, here is how we discovered happiness and how we scaled it to 90+ countries.

CHAPTER 6. DISCOVERING HAPPINESS

It was a rainy bank holiday Monday in May 2008. Chris and I ate breakfast (probably a full English) in John Lewis overlooking Cavendish Square Gardens with our amazing partners, Liz and Celeste, before making the short walk to our new office, or "the cupboard", as we nicknamed it.

There we were sitting in an attic above Wimpole Street in London's West End starting our very own business, and we could not have been happier! We were scared and excited, BUT we were free. We had NO CLUE what we were doing, but ignorance can be absolute bliss.

Along the way, we had all the growing pains, trials, and tribulations you would expect from a fast-growing digital marketing agency in the middle of the digital boom. We made loads of mistakes, but we rode the wave created by our tech partners like Google, Amazon, and Facebook. I have purposely not mentioned team members, clients, and suppliers from this period by name for fear of missing people out, but I will be forever grateful to them. There is not a week that goes by when I don't get a message from one of them recounting a funny story from our shared adventure.

As a first-generation immigrant, I wasn't born into money, but I had something way more important than cash, which is a loving family. My family, like many others, were economic migrants who moved to the UK to find work. My mum worked as a cleaner, and on my dad's side my grandparents found bar work.

There are many parts to privilege, but I personally believe that the ultimate privilege in life is having one parent or guardian who unconditionally loves and emotionally supports you as you grow up. In this area of life, I see myself as incredibly privileged.

On any business journey, hundreds of things can and will go wrong in any given month, but support from friends and family gives you the energy to keep moving forward. In that first year, we lived off of Liz's teacher training salary which is a level of support I will never forget. If you start a business without financial backing, you need to make a lot of sacrifices, but I can honestly say that although we had no money, thanks to Liz we were happy.

By the time we sold, merged, and exited that business, we had worked with brands such as M&S, Ralph Lauren, Melia hotels, Hertz, JP Morgan, Vivienne Westwood, Jamie Oliver, Selfridges, VW, BDO, Nissan, Argos, L'Oréal, Uniqlo, Alibaba, White & Case, and Benefit Cosmetics.

As we started to grow and recruit staff, we used Richard Branson's famous quote as a guiding light on what we wanted our culture to be like: **"Clients do not come first**. Employees come first. If you take care of your employees, they will take care of the clients."

We tried and sometimes failed to put employees first, but we always had positive intent in mind. We were young and stupid, but we were trying to build a culture where people could thrive. Sacking rude clients became a strategy that not only improved morale, it energised the company every time we did it.

You really don't know how much a toxic relationship is draining a company's energy until you move on. I suppose the same is right for all types of relationships.

Looking back, I have no regrets despite all the mistakes we made, but what I have learned and taken forward is to move faster when toxicity moves in. When you are trying to run a business, your rational brain tries to reason with you, but deep down in your gut you know when relationships need to end.

We personalised the Branson approach and developed a new statement of "To strive for personal, client, and agency growth", which was something we took very seriously.

Even to this day, ex-employees recite it to me when discussing their new business adventures. Pride isn't a feeling I experience much, but I do feel proud of the amazing team we had at 4Ps. Looking out into the big, wide world and seeing so many of my former employees starting their own businesses or being key parts of highly successful businesses does give me happiness.

The Happiness Index V1

As our marketing agency got bigger, the clients we worked on got bigger, and we found we weren't able to see them as much as we would have liked. Chris was our Customer Service Director and he wanted to know how they were feeling about our service, but, with 25–30 clients on the books and potentially 10–15 relationships in each client, the maths didn't stack up. Our approach was not scaling well, and we needed to do something about it. We were creaking.

At this stage, Chris took a meeting with Caroline O'Keeffe (who is now our CMO at The Happiness Index – hi, Caroline!), and she gave us some really good feedback. Some of the feedback was good in the positive sense, and some of the feedback was good in the constructive sense.

When Chris asked her about how we could get more of a handle on how we were doing, she mentioned her work with NPS (net promoter scores). This led to some thinking, planning, and general head scratching. The two of us sat down with our CTO Matt Stannard, one of the cleverest and nicest humans I know, and tried to figure out if there was a way we could use technology to see how happy our clients were. As often happens when the three of us get in a room, the ideas started flying (good and bad), I suggested that if we were going to do this with clients, then we should do this with our employees and see if there was a correlation or a flow through.

This is a really practical example of how important a mission or vision is. Because we constantly talked about "personal, client, and agency growth", we made the leap of talking about customer voice to employee voice really quickly. In fact, for us, it would have been weird to separate employee and customer sentiment. A mission statement can't just be some fancy words on a wall or in a HR handbook – you need to live and breathe it or rip them up and start again. Don't be afraid to abandon a mission that your heart doesn't resonate with.

We started with a really simple beta product that one member of the team, Ben Millar, nicknamed 'The Happiness Index' (cheers, Ben). Version one (V1) simply asked how happy our employees and customers were. We sent it out to all the great people we were working with at the time, and feedback started flowing in. Some of it was really positive, and some of it wasn't. But ultimately, that was the point – to learn and grow from. We were able to look at the feedback and take actionable steps to improve what we did as an agency.

Gemma Shambler, who worked in our HR team at the time and is now the Head of People at The Happiness Index, says that far from finding the amount of data daunting, she actually found that having large amounts of information and feedback at her fingertips was exciting. As she's naturally someone who wants to fix problems, having potential issues highlighted to her quickly and easily meant that she was able to gain more insight into more people's working lives than she possibly could have done in face-to-face conversations. Not only was she able to identify problems and quickly work through solutions, she was also getting feedback as to whether those solutions were working or not. This meant she could talk to Chris and myself, and the wider leadership team, with authority and take us on the road to learning from, and growing with, our team.

We were now starting board meetings not with the P&L, but with our employee data first. Our customer data then followed through to the P&L and then the balance sheet.

This continual growth mindset really worked for us. The year we launched the programme we did a record sales year, as we did every year following that. Not only were some of our clients asking if they could use it in their companies, but we'd also proved that it worked at 4Ps. It wasn't perfect, but it was giving us really important emotional intelligence at scale.

Based on demand, we decided to spin it out, and so The Happiness Index company was born. It wasn't until our friend from university, Tony Latter, agreed to quit his well-paid job at Axa Insurance, that we formed a completely separate business called The Happiness Index. Tony was in the classic situation of earning a six-figure salary with a gorgeous company car but not being happy. He gave it all up to pursue his and our dream.

My birthday 2014

So, there we were on another May morning, but this time the sun was shining and we were sitting in my dining room in North London. Chris, Tony, and me with my three-year-old daughter Izzy nestled on my lap... This day was also my birthday, which is a good reminder that if you want to start a business, just get going. Don't wait for the perfect day as it will never come.

Tony set to work with our support, and, one year later, he found someone else prepared to work for free on the business and enlisted my brother Patrick Phelan (he's the good-looking, tall, and smart brother), and we were up and running. In our marketing agency, happiness had been a philosophy; but for this business to work we had to turn it into a platform that could scale.

CHAPTER 7. SCALING HAPPINESS

The problem

The Happiness Index started as a pretty simple solution to a very big problem.

We had data to help run our business on everything, BUT we did not have data on two of the most important things in business: our people and our customer sentiment.

British anthropologist Robin Dunbar proposed human beings have a cognitive social limit. He suggests that we struggle to hold relationships with over 150 people. Importantly, though, this breaks down further and it is suggested that we are only able to have what would be described as less than 20 close relationships.

Employee numbers in a business can also be misleading when looking at the Dunbar number. In some of our clients we just deal with the CEO, but, with larger clients, we are often dealing with 15 people on any one project.

Imagine you are a CEO of a business with only 20 employees, but you have 25 suppliers and 75 customers. A company of just 20 employees can quickly have a wider network of customers and suppliers taking it to well over 150 human relationships to maintain.

How can a business be human as it scales?

Freedom to be human

We have a vision, which everyone at The Happiness Index is

working towards, and that is 'freedom to be human'. But what does that mean, and can it scale?

When we started our first company, we knew that there were thousands if not millions of successful companies out there that had flourished without putting their people first. But had they flourished in spite of what we know? If they had treated their employees better, could they have done better?

What freedom to be human means to us is that if you treat your employees like humans, and allow them to be true to themselves, then that's how your company will thrive.

This need to let your employees be their whole and authentic selves at work has been thrown into stark reality by Black Lives Matter. More and more people are becoming aware that people need to be able to bring their full identities to work in order to be happy and productive.

For us, we wanted a vision that our hearts resonated with but was powered by information from our data.

Freedom to be human gave us this blueprint for growth.

Happiness today

Although a lot has changed over the last eight years since V1, a lot has stayed the same. In some respects, how we use the data that we collect from our employees and customers is much the same but with more advanced technology.

Particularly in today's world where video meetings are more acceptable than before, we're constantly trying to evolve the way we work and understand how our employees and customers are feeling. This means that having those human interactions and building relationships is more important than ever.

One of the things about feedback – and this is a partly British thing, but it's true in a lot of places – is that people tend to err on the side of politeness. You may ask people how they feel BUT are they really going to tell you how they feel to your face? Some people will (checkout *Radical Candour* by Kim Scott), but some people find it difficult.

Already your feedback is going to be skewed by a particular

personality group. Collecting feedback in a multi-channel way is also about getting a diverse pool of people to give you their insight. This is why anonymised data is so important and so powerful – because it lets people give their honest feedback and the raw truth. Which is why our technology platform underpins those human-to-human interactions.

This process of collecting data in real time has taught us some valuable lessons. It's easy to think that you need to make high happiness a target. What we've come to realise as we learn more about happiness and humans is that it isn't realistic or healthy to have happiness targets. Humans can't and shouldn't be happy all the time. They have multiple emotional layers, and it's ok not to be happy all of the time. It is as abnormal to be happy all the time as it is abnormal to be unhappy all the time. Remember Eeyore and Tigger from *Winnie-the-Pooh*? Eeyore is constantly down, and Tigger is constantly up. Neither is a role model to aspire to. A healthy human is a bit of Eeyore and a bit of Tigger.

This is why we've taken away our numerical targets as we evolve our own thinking, and instead we aim to be more like Patricia Phelan (my mum) and always be listening. We're always open to feedback and constructive criticism. We want to hear what our people have to say. And we take that data and that feedback, we share it with senior leadership and the board, and we use this to inform our strategy, decisions, and approach.

Can tech really make companies more human?

Technology is moving forward at a dramatic pace. Humanity has never seen transformation at the speed that we're currently seeing, with computing power rising exponentially almost every year.

When we started The Happiness Index, we started with email for data collection, but increasingly we're finding that people want to voice their opinions on their terms. Feedback is happening on social channels and traditional mediums like email and web. But now we're seeing more feedback on mobile, via established channels like WhatsApp and WeChat, but also voice and other apps. This means employees can communicate where they want to be reached; previously it had to be done via company emails or by certain deadlines, but mobile takes this barrier away.

The key shift is allowing people to feedback how and when they want – and in the channel they decide – in an anonymous way. It should be the employee's decision if they want their identity to be aligned to their comment and not the other way around.

Of course, one of the other key developments in modern technology has been Machine Learning. Our team has been able to use AI alongside Machine Learning in order to really understand the human side of the feedback that we receive at The Happiness Index. We are regularly taking in millions of data points in anonymous text, quotes, or verbatim feedback and turning it into something actionable and insightful in real time, and that can't be done without tech to help.

Advances in technology help classify some of this information, assist in doing some of the hard work, and help companies understand their employees on a human level. Of course, this doesn't replace people. Instead, it frees up their time and helps them to spend more time building relationships.

What have we learned from taking The Happiness Index into over 90 countries?

We have always felt that The Happiness Index needed to be a global company. As a vision-based company, we really wanted to reach as many people, as many lives, and as many organisations as we could. This meant that we needed to be in as many countries as we could be. Of course, we've learned quite a lot along the way.

One of the questions we asked ourselves when we started was whether there were any common truths within happiness. And now, working with so many people across the globe, we can say with some level of certainty that there absolutely are.

Tony calls these our "eternal truths"; these elements that are there within each of us, regardless of language, culture, or country, and are important to us as humans.

A few years ago, I met one of the senior creative team from Pixar at the Cannes Innovation festival and he explained to me how much research had gone into understanding global emotions. His challenge to me was to watch any Pixar movie on mute. He explained that through non-verbal communication anyone regardless of their language would be able to follow the emotions of the characters. The best example of this concept can be found in the *Inside Out* movie where Joy, Sadness, Fear, Anger, and Disgust are key characters. The fact Pixar focuses on these global emotions is not a fluke; it is through painstaking research fed into the art of world-class storytelling.

We know that having a sense of belonging – and being able to be who you are – is something that's very important to people across the globe. This sense of belonging is particularly important in the workplace, because no one wants to put on a front and pretend to be someone else in order to progress or to thrive. The energy required to pretend to be someone else at work is a complete waste of resources, and companies that don't realise this are failing not only their staff but themselves. I still find it so weird that companies can get themselves worked up about how long someone takes for a lunch break, but then they are happy for someone to spend eight hours a day expending energy being someone else at work to fit in with some weird made up tightly defined industry norm.

Another similar thread that we see throughout the world in our data is the need for connectedness. We certainly see that there's a desire to be connected to, and create relationships with, co-workers and colleagues, but also to be connected to the purpose of the organisation you're working for.

Global tech challenges
In taking The Happiness Index to a global scale, we've found that there have been some significant challenges. Key examples include the Chinese Firewall, which threw a significant spanner

in the works but actually it isn't as scary as it sounds – our tech team do like a challenge.

Beyond the hyperbole, the main human challenge has been reaching people in hard to reach places. When we look at global companies, we may not only want to reach executives in London offices with fantastic internet access. In one particular example, we needed to also take into account the experiences of tea pickers in a remote part of Sri Lanka. Our team spent time in the tea farms on the mountainsides in the north of the country to understand the working environment.

What we really try to do is engage with people where they are in the way they want to engage. In terms of technical challenges, this is one of the biggest we face because we have to get our technology right in order to reach all of those people. Then there's also the challenge of understanding the nuances of what is being said. This may be about understanding the sentiment behind speech and the way people write, which we can use AI to start to understand, but of course there are also cultural implications.

For example, you may think of emojis as being a relatively global language, but for those people with a Kenyan connection, in their culture, smiling without using your teeth is seen as insincere, and so these are the kinds of nuances that need to be taken into account. If we hadn't spent time on the ground in Kenya, we would have not understood this.

As with many companies, global challenges have forced us to be more creative and to make use of technology to make these connections. As a company who uses technology to help create connection, what we know is that while it cannot and never should try to replace real human connection, it can help.

What is the future of happiness?

Perhaps Gemma Shambler, our Head of People at The Happiness Index, put it best when she said that the question shouldn't be, "'What is the future of happiness?' but 'What is the future of emotions?'". We're all human and humans aren't only happy, they have a range of different emotions, including positive and more negative ones."

What we need to do is incorporate all those emotions into how we work with each other and make it easier and more acceptable for people to let those around them know when they're not as happy as they could be.

How many times have you answered the question "How are you?" with "I'm fine!" without even really thinking about it? We believe that we should be working towards a culture where people can be open and honest about how they're feeling in any particular moment, with their colleagues and peers, but also with management and leadership within their place of work. It should be totally normal for you to ask your aunty over afternoon tea how her mental health is at the same time as admiring her handy scone work (I apologise in advance for this massive aunty stereotype).

Research is showing us that human emotions have natural peaks and troughs, and this is completely healthy and normal. No one is going to be happy all of the time. Particularly at times of stress or change, there is going to be some negative emotion. This could be created by major change from a merger or acquisition, or even patterns that happen more often like tax season or month end when certain teams have more work. All of these things might incur negative emotions which could last for longer or shorter periods of time. The key is to know how people are feeling so you can help where appropriate.

We have observed that today's emotions are tomorrow's performance. Our technology goal is to enable companies to achieve emotional intelligence at scale.

CHAPTER 8.
HAPPINESS BIOLOGY
AND CHEMISTRY

A note of care

In the next two chapters we use the widest range of research sources in the book. As ever, my note of advice is to be careful with all research and question it as you go (including mine).

Let's take a look at what can be learned from the research.

The science bit

We have mentioned neuroscience a few times in this book so far, but let's take a deep dive into the biology and chemistry behind what we learn in those scans.

Although, we often talk about neuroscience as being literally 'brain surgery', actually when it comes to happiness, there are four chemicals we need to know about, and you've probably heard of all of them before. We're going to look at four chemical neurotransmitters: dopamine, serotonin, oxytocin, and endorphin. All four of them are also hormones, but what they do in the rest of the body is very different to what they are used for in the brain. The word hormone comes from the Greek and literally means to set in motion. This makes sense because our bodies use these chemical signals to put us on the right path to get what we need whether that's more sleep or a few more biscuits. Our bodies have developed a blood-brain-barrier, which keeps everything in order – a very useful function because it means that if we really need a poop, we don't also get a rush of joy!

These four chemicals in and of themselves are actually very common. Most animals in the world produce them. In fact, one of the simplest organisms with a nervous system is a microscopic roundworm, measuring just one millimeter long, that despite its tiny size still produces both serotonin and dopamine in order to help it find and digest the bacteria it eats to live on.

A lot of these chemicals are even used for similar functions in the animal world. If you give a lobster a serotonin boost, you make a super confident happy lobster who confidently takes a higher position in their little lobster social hierarchy. Scientists argue that this isn't too different to the role serotonin plays in humans.

Let's have a quick look at the chemicals we need to keep us happy, what they do, and how we can make sure our bodies have everything they need to produce and use them.

Dopamine

Dopamine is a fun one because it's both a neurotransmitter and a hormone. Dopamine specifically plays a part in everything from learning to lactation, perseverance to pain reception, and, of course, mood.

Dopamine is sometimes known as the pleasure hormone, and this is because when our bodies produce a lot of it, we feel enjoyment and reward. We naturally produce dopamine when we're doing things that the body wants us to keep doing, which means typically we produce lots when we're eating delicious food, meeting our goals, and, of course, funky time (I'm British, I can't type the word ***).

Our bodies synthesise dopamine from amino acids, so it's important that we get enough protein in our diets. For those who are cutting down on their meat consumption, make sure you're getting a complete protein source like eggs or soy because you need both tyrosine and phenylalanine in order to create dopamine.

Recent studies have shown that consumption of too much

saturated fat might disrupt the dopamine response.

Serotonin

Serotonin is an interesting chemical, which mostly hangs out in the gut, but don't judge it by the company it keeps. It's also made in the brain where it's a vital neurotransmitter and plays a key role in functions such as sleeping and eating, so some pretty important stuff.

Unfortunately, the only time serotonin gets widely discussed is in the case of SSRIs, which are a family of drugs used to treat depression and anxiety. If you're chronically deficient in serotonin, SSRIs help to alleviate the symptoms which include both depression and anxiety, and sometimes also sleeplessness, by preventing reabsorption of serotonin in the brain.

When your serotonin levels are normal, you'll feel calmer, more focused, less anxious, and happier. In order to produce adequate levels of serotonin, our bodies need plenty of tryptophan. You can get this as a supplement, but you're probably better off consuming more tryptophan-rich foods such as eggs, salmon, turkey, tofu, and pineapple.

Studies have shown that eating tryptophan-rich foods with plenty of carbs will give you a serotonin boost. Yet another reason to load up on roasties with your Christmas turkey and a scientific explanation for the feelings of joy that accompany the Queen's speech!

Oxytocin

Oxytocin is a neurotransmitter like the other chemicals discussed in this chapter, but one with a bit of a reputation because this is the 'love hormone', and it's mostly linked with reproduction. However, this happy little hormone is also linked to trust and relaxation, and increased oxytocin production is linked to the production of both dopamine and serotonin.

As a hormone, oxytocin actually has a wide range of functions, most of which are linked to the family, for example, lactation and labour. However, it's also produced in both men and women when bonding with their child. In the case of men, this is particularly the case when exploring with babies, but both genders produce it when bathing, singing to, or getting skin to skin time with infants. Interestingly, this isn't limited to biological parents, so even if you've not got kids of your own, you can boost your oxytocin levels by babysitting for your friends and family.

Generally, as long as you're eating a healthy balanced diet, you should be able to produce plenty of oxytocin, but topping up your vitamin C may help support production, and magnesium is needed to help your brain process oxytocin. Some preliminary studies have also linked jasmine essential oil and chamomile tea with oxytocin production, so if you enjoy either of these, they're also a good choice, but there's no conclusive proof right now.

Endorphins

The last of our happiness chemicals, and perhaps the best known, is endorphins. Not only did it have a starring role in *Legally Blond* (no spoilers here, though), but most people know that exercising releases this helpful hormone. They're also a natural pain reliever and play a role in a whole host of other functions which scientists are only just beginning to scratch the surface of.

What we do know is that endorphins, like dopamine, are attached to our reward response, which is how our bodies make sure that we do more of the things that we enjoy and are good for us. We also know that endorphins play a key role in socialisation, which evolutionarily was also a key part of our survival as a species.

In addition to producing that post-exercise 'endorphin rush' that we all know and love, endorphins do all sorts of things in your body. They can help with regulating your weight and even help with pain in childbirth!

Like all our other happiness chemicals, endorphins are made from amino-acid chains, so eating plenty of protein from a range of sources – meat, poultry, fish, eggs, dairy, legumes and seeds, and nuts – is key for endorphin production. Excitingly, some of the foods you eat can also stimulate more endorphin production. These include red wine and chocolate, although a banana, while less fun, will also do the job.

In the next chapter, we will discuss how you can use this knowledge at work and in your everyday life.

CHAPTER 9. HAPPINESS PRACTICAL TIPS

All this science is fascinating for a geek like me but useless unless you actually want to put it into practice. With all research I encourage you to set up your own safe tests and report back to The Happiness and Humans Community how you got on. Get involved and add to the research.

The more we can all learn together the better. It's easy to stand back and criticise researchers and scientists, but I recommend you take the hard road by trying to add more research to the debate so we can learn.

Let's try and prove and disprove as much of this data as we can. As we will see later, your happiness will flow into your business and through into your customers and onto the bottom line, so taking care of yourself is actually good for business.

So, let's have a look at some of the ways in which we can begin to make a difference to our own happiness in simple, tangible steps.

Happiness and health

It's easy to think of your mind and your body being separate entities, but there's just one you and taking care of your physical health has direct impacts on your happiness and the performance of your business.

Healthy eating

It's a fact that I am never going to give up eating two-day-old pizza for breakfast; however, eating a little healthier and making sure you get regular, balanced meals can really work wonders for your mental fitness too.

Exercise

I'm not saying you necessarily need to start training for a marathon (I've run a couple of halves and have really enjoyed them, and I can recommend that), but just getting your body moving can really do wonders. When we exercise, we create more endorphins, dopamine, and serotonin. Find something you enjoy and try to stick to it, whether that be jogging, yoga, walks with the dog, or hardcore gym sessions.

Sun

If you can link your exercise to getting a little sun, so much the better. Just sitting and getting some rays on your face for five minutes in the morning can help set you up for the day. Studies have shown that increased sunlight leads to increased dopamine and serotonin creation, and our brains need vitamin D to function properly. That said, as Mary Schmich pointed out in her 1997 essay on how to lead a happier life and popularised by Baz Luhrmann, don't forget to "wear sunscreen".

Fun fact

Sometimes in the winter we can find we're getting to the office before the sun properly rises and leaving after it sets, so getting some sun on a break can help settle our circadian rhythm as well, which promotes a good night's sleep.

I have been a big fan of walking meetings for a long time now. These days I do way more virtual meetings, but I often still plug in some headphones and walk whilst I am chatting.

Sleep

It's easier said than done but getting eight hours of sleep a night really could change your life. You all know the drill – you probably need to plan to spend more than eight hours in bed to make sure you get eight hours of sleep. Consider turning screens off an hour before bedtime, and limit coffee consumption in the afternoon. The amount of sleep we all need differs but getting serious about your sleep really can boost performance at work.

Happiness and connection

You've heard it before – humans are profoundly social creatures. We're hardwired to gain meaning, solace, and safety in numbers. So, maintaining and building relationships is one of the best ways of making yourself feel happier.

People

We can't always spend as much time with our loved ones as we'd like, but I definitely recommend making it a priority. If you've never taken a phone holiday (or vacation, for our friends across the pond), then I recommend it. Turn your devices off and put them away so you can really spend quality time with the people you care about.

Bonus tip: If you're not physically able to be with the people you care about, ring fence time for phone calls and make them a priority, and, again, give them all your attention. Superstar DJ Norris 'Da Boss' Windross, who appeared on my podcast *Happiness and Humans*, thinks that listening is the key thing when it comes to building relationships, and I have to say I agree.

Physical connection

Getting some physical affection from your friends and family is shown to boost the chemicals which make us feel better. Holding hands or a comforting hug are shown to increase dopamine and oxytocin levels drastically.

Sex

Sex makes you happy. Nothing else to add.

Food

Cooking and eating together promotes the production of oxytocin and breeds trust and relaxation. This is a great tip if you're trying to get closer to your work colleagues, as eating together is the perfect icebreaker. Now you have scientific proof that those lunchtime meetings in your favourite local restaurant are chemically making you closer to your team.

And don't worry – if you work remotely this can still work. For instance, in our office we have a team *Great British Bake Off* competition.

Colleagues
Make sure you build relationships with the people you work with too. We can spend over eight hours a day with our colleagues, and you're probably going to enjoy the time more if you are working with people you like and care about. Make time to find out about what makes the people you work with tick. Not only will this make them happier, but it will also help you.

Animals
If you can't connect with people around you as much as you'd like, connection with animals can help build happiness. If you don't have your own pet, perhaps you can offer to take a friend's fluffy friend for a walk or visit a local farm or petting zoo. Or call my mum and dad and see if you can pop round for a farm tour.

Nature
Connecting with nature might seem a little crazy, but some experts believe that 'forest bathing' should be prescribed on the NHS. Kicking through leaves, listening to birdsong, and, yes, tree hugging, can all make you feel *statistically* happier. So, there we go – get out there and spend some time in nature.

Happiness and mindset
As well as making sure we're getting all the physical benefits we've discussed, there are also ways of thinking that are going to make a world of difference to how happy you feel.

Savouring
Taking notice of all the wonderful things in our lives can make an immediate difference to our happiness. Rather than being distracted, we can really try to be present and enjoy the good things in life. Stop to actually enjoy the hug from your child or partner or the warm cup of morning coffee.

Sharing

It can help to share your joy, particularly with those close to you. Plastering everything across Instagram may not make you happier but talking about the good things in your life might. Plus, telling your friend about the amazing holiday you had in Ibiza will make you feel closer and is proven to extend your enjoyment of your trip.

Gratitude

We will see more of this in Chapter 13 and it might seem a little twee to write down things you're grateful for, but actually the science shows that those who write down a couple of things they're grateful for each day are happier. The more you practice paying attention to and being grateful for the good things in your life, the more you'll notice them.

Celebrating the wins

One of the easiest ways to make yourself happier is to hack your dopamine response by celebrating the wins. Break your big tasks up into small chunks and celebrate each step on the way to your goal. Of course, it's also important to celebrate the bigger wins – take the time to really enjoy reaching goals and feel proud of yourself and others for getting there.

Bonus tip: This counts double for celebrating wins with your team. Whether you've met a small goal or a big milestone, you've achieved it together, and, as such, it should be celebrated together. Think about the ways in which you can give praise and thanks to the members of your team for achieving small things, but also take time out of the day to celebrate the big things too.

Self-care

Self-care is a phrase that's being used more and more these days, and sometimes it can get a bit of a bad rap as being all bubble baths and cakes. However, it's important to give yourself a break, whether that's a long hot shower or cuddling up on the sofa with your kids to watch *The Sound of Music*.

Bonus tip: Self-care could also mean getting those pesky 'adult' jobs out of the way so they're not hanging over your head and causing extra stress – making a doctor's appointment to see about the knee that's been hampering your sports game or sorting through the overflowing pile of post on your kitchen table can make you feel a lot lighter, and achieving something small should give you a dopamine hit!

Happiness and leisure time

We often feel happiest when we're doing something we love in our spare time, but what we choose to do with our time off can actually have a big impact on how happy we are long term.

Group exercise

Studies show that exercising with others has a huge impact on our production of a range of happiness hormones. You could join a local sports league, or start a team with work colleagues, or you could head out for a lunchtime walk with teammates.

One of our clients recently implemented team workouts where they make time for their own team version of a Joe Wicks workout.

Bonus tip: Yoga is a particularly good form of exercise when it comes to happiness, so perhaps you could start going to classes with some friends or join a virtual workout.

Art

Not picked up a paintbrush since school? Making art or music can have a positive impact on your mental fitness. Not only is it a good way to release some of your emotions and focus entirely on something in a mindful way, but it also helps us release endorphins. You don't even have to produce anything particularly high quality to get these benefits!

Spa days

It may sound obvious to you that going to the spa will help you feel happier. But there's actually some science behind this! Both spending time in the sauna and getting a massage have been shown to have an effect on endorphin production, so this is definitely something to bear in mind when you're planning your next holiday.

Acupuncture

A form of medicine which has been used for centuries in China, acupuncture is widely used by GPs and pain clinics in the UK. Largely used to treat chronic pain, studies have also shown that acupuncture is effective when used to treat stress, and even depression and anxiety. Acupuncture also boosts your production of endorphins!

Hypnosis

Hypnosis is an interesting area of study, and there's an increasing body of literature which looks at its effects on everything from addictions to anxiety. Studies indicate that hypnosis can have an effect on your control over your emotions and can potentially help strengthen "happy pathways".

Essential oils

Scientific studies have found evidence to support the idea that essential oils can be a great mood booster and even help alleviate stress and the symptoms of anxiety. You can use any scents that make you smile, but oils that are often used for their relaxing or mood boosting properties include lavender, chamomile, and citrus.

TV choices

Comedy is often the number one choice when it comes to picking to watch something to make you happier, but actually anything that gives us a strong emotional reaction will also work. Studies show that watching sad or emotional movies increases your endorphin production.

Mindfulness and meditation

One of the most well researched and mainstream of the suggestions on this list is mindfulness. Mindfulness has become super popular recently possibly because it's also one of the most effective and is linked to an increase in all your happiness chemicals. Studies have shown mindfulness to have a range of great benefits including reduced stress, increased immune response, better working memory, and generally increased wellbeing.

For those with kids, I highly recommend a children's book called *Happy* by Nicola Edwards that I read with Izzy and Fred. I love this book as it is a light introduction for children to mindfulness.

Happiness and mental health

Happiness is a very personal thing, and all of the studies and practical tips mentioned above are applicable if you're a healthy person with normal levels of mental fitness. However, if you're struggling with poor mental health, you should always seek professional medical advice. While practical tips like the ones mentioned above may help support you, this should not replace getting care from a licensed therapist, counselor, or psychotherapist.

Therapy

There are lots of different kinds of therapy available, some through the NHS and some privately. If you're feeling less happy than usual, or have been feeling down for a long time, this is often the first port of call. Many people find talking therapy useful, and there are lots of different models available. CBT is very popular, but there are plenty of other options such as Transactional Analysis and EDMR, so if you find you don't click with what you try first, talk to your GP.

Medicine

Although there's often a stigma attached to taking medicine for poor mental health, there really shouldn't be. Plenty of people find taking medicines, as prescribed by a doctor or health professional, makes it easier to manage symptoms and lead happy and fulfilling lives, and that's what's important.

CHAPTER 10. HAPPINESS AT WORK: CONTEMPORARY PHILOSOPHY AND EVIDENCE

We've looked at traditional philosophers and their take on happiness. Now I want to introduce you to a new bunch of smart people who have done a whole lot of thinking about the workplace.

I'm lucky enough to work with, talk to, and learn from these people, and I want to introduce you to their ways of thinking about happiness.

Let's dive in and have a look at how ideas about happiness can be directly translated into the world of work.

Happiness and your employees

If you've ever been on any business social network, you've probably seen posts ranting about an individual's feelings about beer fridges, foosball tables, and edgy interior design. Either they love it, or they hate it. But is there more to employee happiness than Friday drinks, playing pool, and having bean bag chairs in meeting rooms?

Arguably, these things do make people happy, and it's important that your team get a chance to let their hair down and relax. However, the thing with happiness, argues Henry Stewart, Founder and Chief Happiness Officer of Happy Ltd, is that it's not about the fleeting in-the-moment stuff that brings people joy, but rather ongoing markers of wellbeing. This means that he doesn't believe you can make your employees happy all the time – or rather you can't make them joyful all the time – but instead you should focus on creating an environment that fosters wellbeing.

Henry founded Happy 32 years ago, with the mission to learn how to create a happy workplace and to spread that information. Now they help organisations create happy workplaces through training and consultancy. He argues that a trust-based environment is more profitable and more effective on any measure. Anecdotally, he has seen that creating a culture where people are positive and supportive, and aren't succeeding at the expense of others, has meant that his clients enjoy working with him. He believes that if you want happy customers, you're not going to get there with unhappy staff.

Again, it's not about a constant state of working bliss; in fact, at Happy, Henry aims to have people enjoying their work 80% of the time. Above all, he wants to empower his employees and give them freedom, trust, and autonomy. Henry argues that it's these factors which are going to bring about more lasting happiness and wellbeing, more so than the best planned blow-out summer party.

Happiness and the individual
Whether you're a mid-level manager, a founder, or a CEO, the key to increasing the happiness of your employees is how happy you are yourself. Happiness, then, starts with the individual, and, once you've started with one person, you can keep building on this success.

Raj Nayak, a happiness philosopher who we work with in India, believes that he can't make people be happy. He argues that people have to do this for themselves, but the company he runs, Happiness.me that is powered by The Happiness Index, can help guide the process of building happiness. Raj works on the belief that happiness begets happiness, and that the more happy people you have in your company, the more energy and productivity you will have. But just as he cannot make you happy, you also cannot force your people to be happy; instead, you must build systems and a culture which encourage happiness.

Raj draws a distinct difference between happiness and pleasure, and he argues that happiness isn't in the big things, but in the small moments. Raj has three main pillars for happiness: empathy, transparency, and communication. For Raj, happiness is not something that happens overnight, but it's something that companies should be constantly working on. Above all, Raj believes that investing in employee happiness is investing in the biggest assets companies have – their people.

Happiness and the boardroom

Once you've started with your own happiness, the next step is to start building happiness in the rest of the company. There are lots of ways in which you can do this, but one of the most powerful and impactful is to start by creating happiness in the boardroom and allowing that to filter down throughout the company.

This is an approach that Louisa Pau, an experienced coach and mentor, takes. She started with her own experience of creating and selling an ad agency while having four children, which she says nearly killed her, and now she works with other founders and CEOs to give them a different journey. Not only is Louisa a hands-on, practical expert, but she also thinks carefully and intelligently about the ways in which relationships and behaviours within the boardroom affect the wider company.

When it comes to the boardroom, Louisa believes that if there's toxicity and fractured relationships on the board, then this will inevitably filter down to the wider company and reduce happiness and efficiency overall. She argues that when everyone in a meeting is happy, they have hormonal and physiological balance, increasing their ability to make effective and efficient decisions.

Louisa believes that boards cannot create purpose, engagement, and, ultimately, happiness, without looking at themselves. She recommends really simple steps to start modelling happiness in board meetings such as modelling positive signals, starting meetings with success, and concluding the meeting with five minutes of silent contemplation on what has been said.

Happiness and conscious leadership

Improving relationships and positive behaviours in the boardroom is the first step. This will then need to be translated down throughout the company.

For this we turn to one of my favourite thinkers on leadership and author of *The Conscious Effect*, Natasha Wallace. Natasha uses her years of experience in HR to help leaders realise their full potential by adapting the framework she lays out in her book. It all starts with a few guiding principles. Firstly, she calls on leaders to be 'Awake' or self-aware, i.e. understanding their own biases and programming. Next, with 'Growing', leaders must understand the extent to which they have a growth mindset and a focus on their strengths and coaching those of others. The third principal is 'Purpose', which should be a higher purpose than making money, and then aligning others to that purpose. Then comes 'Togetherness', and bringing in psychological safety and inclusion, to help people be themselves around their colleagues. Lastly, there's 'Resilience', and maintaining a positive mindset and balancing the internal and external.

Natasha argues that having a happy leader is key to the performance of the team. That's not to say that leaders need to be super cheerful and bounding around, but that happiness comes with a certain level of calm and focus. This can only bring positive energy to the team and create a beneficial and productive atmosphere for the team to work to the best of their ability.

Happiness and HR

In our database, HR professionals often rank the lowest for happiness. We work with HR leaders day in, day out, and we know that they're a vital link to bringing a human element to your plans to improve the happiness of your company. In fact, many of you reading this might be in both leadership and HR positions.

Natasha Wallace knows from her HR experience that it's key to have the HR team on board when it comes to spreading happiness through organisations. Our research has found that HR might not be the happiest people in a company, and Natasha puts this down to the fact that, particularly in the turbulent times we find ourselves in, HR often has to deal with a lot of the emotional work in an organisation. For example, they may have to be involved with redundancy and furlough processes, and also deal with members of your team who are struggling on a day to day basis. These can be very impactful on HR team members' mental health, particularly for those who have gone into HR because of their empathetic nature and their love of people.

In our 2019 study that looked specifically into the happiness of HR professionals, we found while The Happiness Index recorded a benchmark of 7.7, HR professionals rated their overall happiness at work at 6.8 on average. Commitment to helping the organisation succeed was cited as one of the most significant factors providing HR professionals with happiness (8.4), followed by how well they get on with others at work (7.8). The lowest two factors were both related to learning and development, specifically satisfaction with the opportunity to progress their careers (5.8), and the amount of training on offer (6.1).

Happiness, music, and flow

Flow is a well-studied area of happiness. It means to be completely absorbed in a task so that you don't even notice time passing, and it is the kind of state of happiness that Confucius introduced earlier. Flow is important when we think about happiness at work, because often flow and task engagement are studied together in the case of job happiness.

With a background in garage music, Norris 'Da Boss' Windross relates much of happiness back to music, meditation, and flow. For him, DJing is about bringing a group of people together in one rhythm, and, so, one flow. He believes that whether you're bringing together a group of people to move together in dance to the same beat, work on an important project, or achieve a common goal, there's a little bit of magic in this sense of flow. As I see it, ultimately, this is what leadership is all about – bringing individual and unique humans together to unite them under a common purpose.

When we move outside of the scientific definition of flow, there's also a sense of a movement of energy within the term. Norris believes that as we move through life, each of us brings different energy, and different vibrations, and these energies and vibrations are projected through people's auras. These can be felt in meeting rooms, client calls, and networking opportunities, and, arguably, this is what we were missing during lockdown – the tangible energy of being in the same room as people and feeding off their energy. However, as radio DJs the world over have demonstrated, it's possible to project these qualities even remotely, and Norris argues we need to think about ways in which we can tap into those energies while we work from home.

Happiness and branding

When it comes to happiness, making your employees and board happier will not only make your customers happier and make you more money, but it will also make it easier for potential new customers to find you.

Increasingly, we're seeing brands using their own (happy) staff in their brand advertising. This is true for both big brands, such as Amazon, and smaller brands, such as Montezuma chocolates. This may be linked to increasing evidence that customers will consider boycotting brands who don't treat their employees well. For instance, in 2020, there have been calls to avoid Amazon in the US, and brands like Boohoo in the UK faced a backlash when allegations emerged regarding treatment of factory workers by some of their suppliers. Websites such as Glassdoor have opened up culture so the entire outside word can take a peep behind the curtain. No longer can culture and brand be separated. Like it or loathe it, sites like Glassdoor are not going away, and they will impact how your brand is perceived.

Branding expert Brandon James thinks that, ultimately, this human face in advertising comes back to the need for authenticity. There's mounting evidence that, as Brandon says, the old adage that people buy from people is true, and he points to the advent of social media as a proof point of this. During the pandemic we saw that small businesses and solo entrepreneurs have been able to leverage our higher screen time to build an audience online and through social media and amass orders on an unprecedented scale.

Brandon argues that happiness is the thing that brings people together the best. This is because happiness is shareable and sparks loyalty, and it is something that you can continue to relate to, watch, and remember for a long time.

When we think about the idea that happiness is contagious, in the way that Raj and Louisa discussed, then this spreads easily and makes marketing easier. In a world driven by social media, it's this shareability, the contagion, and, dare I say it, the virality of happiness that makes for an excellent branding strategy.

CHAPTER 11. EMPLOYEE HAPPINESS: RESEARCH AND EVIDENCE

We live in a world where phrases like 'post-truth era' get thrown around all the time. Leaders are fact-checked by Twitter, and we're increasingly being told that the general public don't trust experts. Between the climate change deniers, and conspiracy theorists, it can sometimes feel like no one trusts data anymore. But, in the case of happiness, the data, science, and experts tell a compelling story around the importance of employee engagement and creating happiness in the workplace, both for individuals and for the business.

Let's have a look at the studies and science from some of the leading data experts in this field to get to the bottom of the impact happiness can have in the workplace.

Happiness at work

As we're doing this the scientific way, before we begin looking at various studies and reports, we should begin by defining some terms. For this we'll turn to a really helpful analysis by Cynthia Fisher out of Bond University. Her 2009 review gathers together much of the research and thinking that had been completed up until that point and creates a useful framework on which we can build our scientific understanding of happiness in the workplace.

Fisher starts her paper by drawing on work that suggests, as we've seen before, that hedonic happiness is unsustainable without *eudaimonic* aspects of happiness. She argues that research shows that they are correlated and so there is no need to make a distinction between the two in empirical scientific study.

When it comes to happiness specifically at work, Fisher defines three discrete ways of measuring this: transient, personal, and unit level happiness. Examples of transient happiness at work could be flow state, task enjoyment, and emotion at work. This is seen as separate from personal happiness, which includes measures such as engagement, job satisfaction, and organisational commitment. Lastly, there are larger measures of unit happiness, or the happiness of a group of employees is discussed, i.e. morale or group mood. But Fisher argues that the ways of collecting this data are flawed as usually individual happiness is measured and then averaged over the group.

Fisher's review of the research shows that there are many factors which influence happiness at work. She lists a number of studies and the different impacts they have; for example, charismatic leadership is strongly related to job satisfaction and organisational commitment. She also goes on to discuss the impacts of happiness within the workplace and speculates that "evidence suggests that the 'happy–productive worker hypothesis' may be more true than we thought". Let's have a look at the data which backs up this view.

Happiness and performance

Employee engagement is something we've touched on a number of times in this book with Jeremy Dawson. Here he gives a really clear breakdown of what it actually means and how it affects employee happiness. He explains there are three separate components of employee engagement. The first is motivation, or psychological engagement, which he believes is the most closely linked to happiness. The second is around involvement, i.e. speaking up and being included in key decision making. Lastly, the third component is advocacy, or how willing individuals are to encourage others to come work for, or be a client of, the organisation for which they work.

One of the key areas of study that happiness philosophers and practitioners have looked at is the link between happiness and performance. Many people want to make their employees happy because they know it's the right thing to do, but sometimes it requires more proof to make boards, and other key stakeholders, sit up and take notice. This, then, has become a point of research for scientists as they aim to put data behind the gut feeling. This is because sometimes gut feelings can be misleading. There are plenty of examples out there of times where your gut feeling would be counterproductive – Alex Edmans, economics professor at London Business School, gives the example of a child with diarrhoea. Although you may feel you shouldn't give them water, in fact they need more water, so they don't get dehydrated.

Happiness and productivity

Although there have been many studies that show that happiness and performance are linked, scientists wanted to prove that there was a causal as well as correlational relationship between the two. Scientists wanted to show that the increased performance seen in happy employees was caused by this happiness, and not because, for example, great performance made people happier.

In a study out of Saïd Business School, University of Oxford, Jan-Emmanuel De Neve and his colleagues set out to answer this question: what is the impact of employee happiness on productivity? The experts looked at employee productivity within sales teams at large BT call centres. BT is one of the largest private employers in the UK and gave a good view onto varied workplaces, as the study covered 11 different locations.

The study, published in October 2019, showed that employee happiness had a direct impact on productivity. In particular the researchers found a direct correlation between poor weather and a decrease in employee happiness, as well as a subsequent impact on employee performance. This could be seen in a variety of measures including the number of calls made, how closely employees stuck to their workflow and how many calls were converted to sales. Their findings supported an earlier study by Ward et al., which showed that higher wellbeing at work is correlated with more business-unit level profitability.

Happiness and employee burnout

Employee burnout is an increasingly important threat to the happiness of our workforce. Research shows that 48% of UK workers have experienced burnout rising to 66% of US workers. Getting a handle on this can be a big driver in ensuring happiness in yourself and/or in your employees. Cutting-edge research out of the London Business School from Laura Giurge could have the answer. She researched the impacts of giving employees two hours a day to focus on important but non-urgent tasks, compared to others who were not given this time. Those in the group who were given what she calls pro-time, were encouraged to switch phones to airplane mode, not answer emails, and really focus on their important tasks. Following just six weeks of pro-time four days per week, Giurge and her team were able to record a decrease in burnout of 6%. Giurge hypothesised this would increase over time.

But what to do if you are feeling like you're slipping towards burnout? Sometimes it's tempting to think you'll have to do something extreme like a big holiday abroad, or hours in bed, or a full on silent retreat to get ourselves back on track. In actual fact, Giurge's research has shown that what she calls "active leisure" is the best way to get your work mojo back. This would involve doing things like spending time with friends and family, volunteering, or enjoying hobbies. She recommends treating your weekend like a holiday and really enjoying it. One of the tricks Giurge uses is to make a list of things she may want to do at the weekend, so that she really thinks about how she wants to spend her time, and doesn't just let her days off slip by.

Giurge understands the difficulty of turning off from work. Despite knowing her own research really well, she sometimes struggles to take a break from work herself. I too know that when you really love the work, sometimes you just want to crack on, but you'll be doing yourself and your team a disservice if you do.

Culture and brand are the same thing

It was always a myth that brand and culture are separate things, but employee review websites like Glassdoor have put that argument to bed. You can ignore Glassdoor all you like, but bad reviews on it are going to impact how your brand is perceived. It will put off talent joining you and customers will have a window into your organisations.

Andrew Chamberlain and Daniel Zhao from Glassdoor concluded in their paper, "The Key to Happy Customers? Happy Employees": "There is a strong statistical link between employee well-being reported on Glassdoor and customer satisfaction among a large sample of some of the largest companies today. A happier workforce is clearly associated with companies' ability to deliver better customer satisfaction."

Happiness and profit

Ultimately, companies need to prove that they're profitable. This means sometimes it's hard to persuade boards and other stakeholders to invest in employee or even board-member happiness without strong data which shows the link between happiness and profit. Luckily, there's loads of research which shows the link is really strong.

Alex Edmans has studied the relative performance of companies who invest in their workforce versus those who do not. He looked at the list of the 100 best companies to work for in the US, controlling for industry, performance size, and so forth, as well as ensuring that he was looking at causation rather than correlation. His research found that, over a 28-year period, these companies had stock returns that beat their peers by 2.3–3.8% per year, or 89-184% cumulative. He argues that this means that companies shouldn't view their workers as a cost centre but as an asset. His data shows that his findings hold true across all industries and all levels and functions.

Edmans takes this research further and uses the image of a pie to stand for the value a company creates. He argues that if companies give slices of the pie to investing in their employees, reducing carbon footprint, or spending on customer welfare, this doesn't diminish, but rather grows, the pie. For example, rather than squeezing as much effort out of people as possible, and viewing them as a resource, we should instead see them as Raj does – as an asset. This shift in mindset allows business leaders to not only value and increase employee happiness, but also increase their profits.

Happiness and the bigger picture

As we saw in Chapter 2 while looking at philosophies of happiness, sometimes happiness can start with one person. Although you, like Louisa Pau, might anecdotally think that starting with happiness programmes from the top will work, there's actually data which backs up this observation.

Specifically, we're going to be looking at the idea of emotional contagion. Emotional contagion is the idea that one person's emotions can directly impact the feelings and behaviours of others. The term was first coined in 1993 by the psychologists Elaine Hatfield, John Cacioppo, and Richard Rapson. Many psychologists and other scientists have completed research in this area, and it's a fascinating rabbit hole of interesting reading, but the most relevant to our purposes is the work by Sigal Barsade. A professor at Wharton Business School, Sigal Barsade has been researching emotions, emotional connections, and leadership throughout her entire career.

In a 2001 study, Barsade shows that in small groups, work output could be manipulated by one member of the group displaying certain moods. In "Mood and Emotions in Small Groups and Work Teams", Barsade explores the idea that the mood of one person in a group could affect the whole team. She had one actor in a meeting or room display certain behaviours or emotions to show that these behaviours and emotions spread to the whole group and directly impact outcomes and performance within the meeting. Not only this, but her research also shows that the members of the group didn't know it was happening. In short, leaders modelling behaviours, attitudes, and emotions within meetings will have a much bigger and more far reaching impact on organisational life than you might expect, as Louisa accurately assessed.

Barsade's 2018 paper, "Emotional Contagion in Organizational Life", builds on her earlier research in the area of emotional contagion. The study collates 25 years of research to provide a holistic framework for emotional contagion and its effects on everything from processes and outcomes to customer attitudes. Here we can see the full extent of the impact of emotional contagion – not only can changing the emotions within your organisation make your workforce happier, it can also make your customers happier as well.

Happiness and relationships
While it's important that people enjoy the work they're doing and find it meaningful and fulfilling, it's equally, if not more, important that they have good relationships with their colleagues. This is one of the things that has become particularly evident during the pandemic. As everyone got used to working from home, the one thing that many found they were missing most wasn't the commute, the free breakfasts, or the ergonomic office chairs – although people did miss those things. People were missing their colleagues.

Social support is very important to performance. At The Happiness Index, we've seen that the data shows an 'emotional deficit', which impacts employee happiness, and we often see that one of the bigger factors in employee happiness is appreciation. Jeremy Dawson cites a study that suggests that there should be a ratio of 3:1 of positive to negative feedback. Considering our own data at The Happiness Index puts feedback in the top tier of important things that need to be present for employees to be happy, this 3:1 advice is really important.

This feedback should come from a variety of sources, including managers and supervisors, but also peers, colleagues, and clients. Being able to connect with people is also key, Dawson says that the key factor is the human relationship. Essentially, you need to be able to empathise with the person you're thanking and understand where they're coming from and what they've done and having that real connection is the difference between heartfelt appreciation of someone's work and going through the motions.

Want to study wellbeing at Yale for free?

I can't go into the full detail of all the happiness research and data out there – this book would just get too long! If you're interested in immersing yourself further into some more of the wide range of data available and the fascinating scientists who are working on this area, I would highly recommend looking into the course "Science and Well-being", formulated by Laurie Santos, a professor at Yale University.

Originally called "Psychology and the Good Life", it quickly became one of Yale's most popular courses – at its height, one in four Yale students had taken the course. Santos blends science and practical tips into her 10-week course. Early on in the course she mentions the 'GI Joe Fallacy', which states that knowing is half the battle; Santos advocates for learning the theory and putting it into practice simultaneously.

In 2020, during the global pandemic, Santos and Yale University made the entire course free to access on Coursera. At time of writing, over 2.5 million students have enrolled.

CHAPTER 12. HAPPINESS: PRACTITIONERS AND EVIDENCE

When it comes to happiness at work, no one is more aware of the key role it plays than our happiness practitioners. They are on the frontline and they are using the research and philosophy discussed in the last two chapters (Chapter 10: Happiness at Work: Contemporary Philosophy and Evidence and Chapter 11: Employee Happiness: Research and Evidence).

The importance of happiness at work

As we discussed, certain companies, such as tech companies are frequently attacked in the press for not putting their people first. However, as Jenn Lim, Founder and CEO of Delivering Happiness (our partners in the US), points out this isn't unique to tech companies in general. Although, intellectually, people know that treating employees well is a key facet to financial performance, sometimes top execs are still motivated by the wrong things. Jenn argues that these incentives need to change, particularly in terms of short-term stock price protection.

Companies can use a variety of words to connote the idea of happiness, such as wellbeing, thriving, flourishing, etc., and this can be manifested in a variety of ways too. For example, Jenn tells the story of a building company in Egypt which redesigned their entire headquarters in order to physically embody their values and purpose, and to give dedicated space to wellbeing and happiness.

Jenn recommends starting with a commitment from senior stakeholders, and then start with top-down alignment, as we discussed in Chapter 10. But, in terms of practicality, she also recommends a bottom-up approach. This, in her experience, leads to more practical steps which are immediately applicable in your specific organisation. Having dedicated ambassadors who already embody your values and purpose will help to reward, incentivise, and provide ownership for cultural action.

Happiness and education

While on the surface recruiting from the best universities makes sense and sounds great in a sales brochure, in reality it often leads to a lack of diversity and a dearth in opportunities that a team from diverse backgrounds can offer. Because of this inbuilt reverence for academic learning, innate talent, experience, or other factors which may make up someone's authority on different subjects may be overlooked.

In France, they have an acclaimed and prestigious higher education system called the *grandes écoles,* which accept students based on their national ranking in written and oral exams, recruiting the top 5%. In the UK and US, we see some firms who give preference to Oxbridge and Ivy League graduates as they are seen as being more intelligent. Malene Rydahl, author of *Happy as a Dane*, has observed that in France, those who have studied at *grandes écoles* are often given more of a voice than others in their companies. The downside of this is those who haven't been to those schools may feel like their voices are being ignored and the company loses valuable input.

It's important to remember that everyone in your company deserves a voice including people from top universities. I personally still hire people from top universities, but it's worth remembering that in order to ensure that everyone in your organisation is able to feel appreciated and like they're part of your company's mission, you need to make space for everyone's ideas and opinions.

In 2015, Ernst & Young actually removed the degree threshold from their graduate recruitment stating there is "no evidence" success at university correlates with achievement in later life.

At 4Ps Marketing, our previous company, we followed suit when we assessed the reasoning behind EY's change, and I would never go back. We have the same approach at The Happiness Index today. We believe the innovation and creativity that a team of people from diverse backgrounds bring is a much more exciting prospect than seeking safety in recruiting from a few select universities.

Happiness and performance

In 2012, Google started a research group called the Aristotle Project to try to find out what makes the perfect team. It was clear that some teams performed better than others, but it was hard to figure out what made those teams so much more effective. In the end, Google came up with an answer which sat remarkably close to the work of Amy Edmundson, a professor at Harvard Business School. She coined the term "emotional safety" in 1999, and it is this concept which sits at the heart of Google's findings when it comes to high-achieving teams.

It seems that in teams where everyone trusts the other group members, performance is higher. There are a number of factors to this. Team members should feel free to be themselves; share even their craziest ideas; discuss errors or things going wrong freely; ask questions, particularly when they don't understand a process or idea; and share when they don't feel like they are the best person to complete a task. In short, a team where members feel they can communicate safely, without worrying about judgment or embarrassment.

Malene Rydahl argues that it is this that is key to innovation. When people feel that they are able to share and suggest new ideas, regardless of whether they fall directly within their job roles or not, this is when new and exciting ideas are brought to the table. This is when innovation happens. For Malene, innovation is about daring to be different. She argues that the data shows that when people trust their companies, they're more willing to take risks, and therefore innovate. She argues that for every great idea, there are two bad ideas. For this reason, Malene argues that it's key that companies foster an atmosphere where people can come up with one or even two terrible ideas, and their third idea will be listened to with as much patience, interest, and even enthusiasm as the first two.

Happiness and alignment

One of the key things to maintaining happiness in the workplace is ensuring there is a sense of purpose for your organisation. However, sometimes the case may be that your purpose and that of the place where you work are no longer entirely aligned. Of course, your principles and values change over time, as your life changes, and those of the organisation you work for may also shift. For this reason, it's important to keep your finger on the pulse of your place of work's purpose and mission, but also to make sure you have a strong sense of your own values. This will mean that you're able to quickly spot when you're no longer as aligned with your organisation as you once were.

Malene Rydahl puts this into the terms of a relationship. She describes that although she always strives to be flexible and to stretch her comfort zone, there are certain things that go against her key principles and values. When this is the case, Malene stresses the importance of radically reassessing the relationship you have with your place of work. For example, on one occasion when a company she worked for was making a decision which she did not agree with, Malene told them if this went ahead, she would need to rethink their long-term relationship. Ultimately, the company did not make the decision, which shows the importance of standing up for your own values and beliefs.

Happiness and purpose

Jenn Lim talks about three kinds of happiness: pleasure, passion, and purpose. Each of these has its place, but the most sustainable, and the most relevant to the context of work, is purpose. As Jenn points out, we can spend more than half of our waking hours working, and so it's really important that companies focus on the meaning they bring to their employees. Even in this age where companies are increasingly putting focus on their purpose, this doesn't necessarily mean that this directly transfers to their employees.

When it comes to purpose, Malene gives the example of the Danes (who else?!). In Denmark, seven out of 10 people are happy to pay taxes, which is a very high number. This is because they see paying taxes as part of taking part in the 'project' that is Denmark. They're taking part in creating the welfare state and supporting their fellow Danes, and this is something they're proud to do. Being part of something that is greater than themselves gives them a sense of purpose. When you bring this back to the workplace, we see that when people feel they are getting up and going to work not simply to get a paycheck or pay the bills, they're more engaged, happier, and produce better results. However, a recent Gallup poll suggested that up to 85% of people across the world aren't engaged at work.

Happiness and progress

When I say progress, you might think of finishing big projects or winning large new clients. As humans, it's easy for us to forget about the small wins which make up the path to those bigger things. However, there's something called the progress principle. This states that celebrating the small, everyday wins is something that can have a big impact on people's mood, efficiency, and effectiveness at work. I am personally very guilty of forgetting to do this.

Teresa Amabile and Stephen Kramer, who discovered and literally wrote the book on the progress principle, discovered it by analysing diaries kept by workers. They found that, while there were a number of things that could affect happiness, the one that had the most impact was making progress in meaningful work. This led to them writing *The Progress Principle*. The book takes the 12,000 diary entries they studied and turns this information into a useful guide, with practical tips on how managers can ensure that they give their direct reports everything they need to make the progress they need to have positive inner work lives.

On a practical note, Arlette Bentzen, who helps transform the happiness of companies every day, has found that this principle is one of the most useful to her and brings the best results. She always goes back to this because she knows that while managers want to see performance, and they want people to be more productive, they often forget to talk about the progress that is being made in the process. She argues that in many jobs, you're in the middle of a chain – you might complete your work and deliver it to another colleague, and they might see the project to completion. In these situations, it's key to talk about the hand everyone had in the project.

Even if you're not successful in finishing the project, or winning a large new client, it's also really important to take time to notice and celebrate the things that did go well. Our brains have a negative bias, and so it's easy for us to see the things that have gone wrong, but, oftentimes, there are also numerous things that haven't. Managers and leadership teams need to make sure to take the time to celebrate those things, and point out that, on a larger scale, failure is actually a step towards future wins.

Happiness and your career

Progress doesn't only come at a macro or organisational level; there's also the sense of personal progress which is so important both to your happiness and to those around you. As we've already discussed, if you're in a leadership position, it's key that you're able to project happiness and be yourself, as these are the kinds of behaviours that those around you will model. However, on a personal level, happiness is also very important in a career. Although in earlier chapters we saw that having the perfect high paying job may not bring you as much happiness as you may have thought, aligning with a purpose and building strong relationships will bring you happiness. This will also, according to career coach John Fitzgerald, take you along a path to a great career.

John argues that finding a great career isn't about making the most possible money. In fact, he, like me, has taken several new jobs with pay cuts in order to move closer to his goals and values. I have only switched jobs four times and on all four occasions it has been for a huge pay cut so I could expand my learning.

John describes this as being like a game of 'hot and cold' as a child. You should constantly be assessing whether this move makes you feel like you 'got warmer' towards something that both brings you joy and aligns with your values, but also teaches you something and brings you into contact with people who you enjoy learning and working with.

John also believes that career happiness is a two-way street – that individuals need to take responsibility for their own happiness, to understand their own skills and values, and to look for ways in which they can add value to companies. However, he also argues that companies need to look at employees as individuals.

When it seems that a particular individual has stagnated and is no longer adding value, organisations should look at what skills, passions, and potential the individual has. Then they can assess where they have opportunity within their organisation to help that person align their skills and values with what the organisation needs.

Happiness and diversity and inclusion
Kevin Withane, who is a diversity and inclusion expert, introduced me to the McKinsey report, "Diversity Wins". This report from 2019 looks at 1,000 companies across the world, including

in both the UK and the US, and shows that diversity and inclusion has a direct impact on a company's bottom line.

In fact, the gap in performance between those companies that are the most diverse at board level and those who are least is actually increasing. Kevin believes it's the inclusion here which is at play, where inclusion means that people with diverse backgrounds are being actively retained and included so that they can help build an organisation's success.

Ultimately, Kevin argues that diversity in and of itself isn't linked to happiness, but that equity and inclusion can be. These elements can drive trust, psychological safety, and engagement, and if people feel engaged, that means they're happy and they're enjoying their work. When people turn up to work and don't feel engaged, they're just completing the function. But when people are happy and engaged, they put their soul into it. So, diversity and inclusion, if done well, will drive happiness, and happiness will drive engagement, which will drive performance.

When it comes to practical steps to ensure progress is made at the board level, Margot Slattery, Global Diversity and Inclusion Officer at Sodexo, suggests starting with the data. She suggests that boards should do a diagnostic and understand what the situation is within their own organisation. There are five key areas to look at: disability, gender, orientation, generation, and race and ethnicity. From there, you need to understand what the data is telling you and what story you are seeing about your own organisation. From here, you need to look at the board, and if you've been working at your diversity and inclusion and it's not translating to the board, then you have a problem. Then you need to start setting tangible actions and goals around what you want your top table to look like, in order to drive the conversation forward.

Happiness and LGBTQ+ rights

Of course, there are many strands to diversity and inclusion, and while race may be a big one to tackle, there are also questions around a number of different facets of people's identities.

When thinking about her life as someone who is LGBTQ+ and wasn't able to be out for a long while, Margot Slattery notes that there is a link between happiness and LGBTQ+ progress. She says that when you can be yourself and you don't have to tell lies, hide parts of yourself, or cover over things, then you're a happier person, and a better person.

While progress is being made, there is, however, a note to be made around issues of gender identity, gender roles, and transgenderism, and that this is where even more progressive societies are falling short. Trying to box people into specific gender identities and roles continues to be a serious issue. Margot particularly sees this in the case of LGBTQ+ people who are forming families and negative reactions from women regarding trans issues, which she finds concerning.

The main advice that can be given to anyone approaching diversity and inclusion, particularly from a position of privilege as a white and/or straight person, is to ask the uncomfortable questions. You're always better off asking the question and getting to understand the individuals concerned, so that you can understand what is needed and the perspectives within your organisation or network rather than making generalisations. Of course, these conversations need to be had in the right place, at the right time, and in the right ways, but from these conversations you can build tangible actions. Margot describes this as a block by block approach which allows you to build upon small amounts of progress.

Happiness and tough decisions

Life is never plain sailing, and we know that there will always be times regardless of the situation or the wider political and global spheres, that companies have to make tough decisions.

Nicola Pearcey, UK and European President at Lionsgate, argues that it's a leader's job to balance employee wellbeing with tough decisions. Nicola admits that this isn't easy; often a layer of trust is taken away and courage can be reduced when the fear factor of uncertainties is introduced. However, she encourages leaders to double down on these areas that are naturally limited in uncertain circumstances, as they're even more important. The tougher the situation, the more you need to listen.

Nicola also encourages leaders to be vulnerable themselves. When we throw ideas, potential solutions, and our own opinions into the mix, we show others that they can do the same. She also stresses that anyone can be a leader during unstable times – she argues that a leader is anyone who's willing to take others on the journey, and so any of us can take on this role of trying to rebuild positivity.

Happiness and the law

You may have gathered at this point that employee happiness is very important to me, and so I wanted to find out how this intersects with the law. I spoke to employment law expert Louise Lawrence about how happiness and the law intersect both in the UK and in the US, to find out to what extent employers are legally obligated to ensure their employees are happy.

What I found out was that, although the Declaration of Independence does guarantee US citizens' right to pursue happiness, this is a moral standard and not a legally binding document. Here in the UK, we do have legal standards such as the implied duty of mutual trust and confidence, which means that an employer cannot act in a way that is likely to destroy or seriously damage the relationship between the employer and employee.

This covers obvious things like workplace harassment, but also things like if an employer gives too much work to an employee but doesn't support them in completing it. However, similarly as to in the US, this doesn't cover the actual happiness of the employee. Louise explained to me that this is because happiness is a subjective feeling and so hard to bring into law.

However, there are a number of ways in which companies and organisations can commit to making it a legal requirement to look after their employees. These include programmes like the Mindful Business Charter, which banks and law firms can sign up to to commit to making their workplaces better places to work for their employees. Similarly, B Corps is a way of amending the articles of association for a business which means that other elements such as environmental concerns and employee wellbeing are given equal prominence to financial returns. Another potential option could be a 'happiness charter', but we'll come back to this idea in the final chapter.

Happiness and nature

Of course, happiness extends outside the workplace, and sometimes the workplace extends outside into nature. Now, we're not just talking about going on a wilderness retreat and then coming back and trying to reverse engineer learnings back into the workplace. But as Tabitha Jayne, Director and Lead Coach of Earthself, explains, we're actively looking to embed the lessons we can gain from nature into their workplace.

Social phycologist Erich Fromm coined the term biophilia, a psychological orientation for attraction to all that is alive. According to Tabitha, studies have shown that time spent in nature can boost your mood, creativity and even decrease time spent in hospital. The next space for research, according to Tabitha, is that organisations need to consciously include biophilia in their organisational design.

Tabitha explained that a natural antidepressant has been found in soil that is said to have a similar effect on neurons that drugs like Prozac provide.

Christopher Lowry, an expert in this area, commented:

The idea is that as humans have moved away from farms and an agricultural or hunter-gatherer existence into cities, we have lost contact with organisms that served to regulate our immune system and suppress inappropriate inflammation. That has put us at higher risk for inflammatory disease and stress-related psychiatric disorders.

Lowry optimistically summed up things by saying, "We are just beginning to see the tip of the iceberg in terms of identifying the mechanisms through which bacteria evolved to keep us healthy. It should inspire awe in all of us."

Tabitha concludes that green spaces around the building and indoor gardens don't go far enough. There needs to be time and space built into daily work life to appreciate and enjoy it. Systems need to be put in place to help people connect with nature, find the beauty in nature, and spend time outside.

Maybe it is the farmer in me, but the research in this section has left me in complete awe of nature. If businesses truly want to reconnect with their employees, they need to understand they can't separate humans from nature, as we are all part of the same system.

CHAPTER 13. THE HAPPINESS INDEX DATA

As Benjamin Disraeli famously said, there are "Lies, damned lies, and statistics", which is probably my favourite quote of all time. I love data, but I always take data with a handful of salt and approach it with a quizzical mind (even my data).

In this chapter, I use a randomised anonymous data sample from The Happiness Index Universe (our database) of approximately 7.3 million data points, from 498,397 employees across 95 countries. We have one of the biggest databases on employee happiness in the world, but I constantly remind everyone not to jump to conclusions. Data is only true in that moment of time.

No data set in the world is 100% accurate, but that doesn't mean we can't learn and advance our knowledge from looking at it.

Picking a first 11 in football is tough, but picking a first 11 from a global database is almost impossible. Here are the 11 bits of insight that I think can help you make your business case for happiness.

What makes people happy?

1a. Relationships with colleagues

We consistently find that the number one influence on employee happiness is the quality of relationships between colleagues.

It's no secret that we humans have a desire to feel connected to one another. It's a basic human need, and one that – when fulfilled – will ensure greater creativity, productivity, and performance. Not to mention the numerous benefits for wellbeing and mental health!

Creating a culture that facilitates personal relationships is key for employee happiness and company culture. It's impossible for organisations to foster a culture of trust if teams and departments work in silos. Promote teamwork and inter-departmental integration to ensure greater collaboration and healthier workplace relationships. You *will* reap the benefits.

1b. Receiving feedback

Many people are surprised when they see how high feedback is on the list of employee happiness.

When leaders have regular, open lines of communication with their people and provide updates around company news and personal performance, it ensures everyone feels like a vital part of the business. Receiving regular feedback and support will help employees understand how their role has an impact on the success of the business. This is essential for their development and cultural and overall business growth.

I highly recommend regular updates to staff around customer successes and failures. Hearing these stories can help remind employees why they do what they do – and further cement how they fit into the bigger picture.

What makes people unhappy?

So, we know the two things that need to be present to make people happy, but what two things create unhappiness if they are missing?

2a. Career opportunities

Our data revealed that employees gave 'career development' their lowest average score of 5.7. This suggests that many are unhappy with the prospects on offer to them. It came as no surprise that younger people (18–30) answered more positively and the scores dropped significantly from the age of 45. This clearly highlights that businesses must keep older workers in mind when thinking about future opportunities.

To demonstrate this correlation, those who scored 7.0 or above for 'feeling valued' rated their career development opportunities as 7.3, and those who scored lower than 7.0 scored their career development as 4.1. This presents a win-win scenario for businesses that want to make their staff feel more recognised and valued... while creating more developed and skilled workers in the process.

2b. Culture eats strategy for breakfast

Culture is the heartbeat of your business, and values are the beliefs and philosophies that guide it. People don't always notice culture and values in the good times, but they certainly recognise if they are missing in the bad times.

If your employees don't align with either, it's no big surprise they won't be happy.

We all have our own personalities that define us and make us unique. Similarly, every organisation has its personality (guidelines, practices, vision, etc.). This is your company's culture. Thriving work cultures facilitate trust, collaboration, and productivity. They also ensure that everyone aligns with the company's values.

Company values are essentially the points of the compass that guide your business. If the values of the individual employee don't align with that of the business, then this will be detrimental for your company culture. Businesses must listen to their staff and empower them to build and contribute towards the culture. Even the best company cultures still have room for improvement.

3. When the going gets easy, the tough get...

Not quite a Billy Ocean lyric, but, in a subset of 150,000 employees, we found that employees don't quit because the job is too hard but because they don't feel challenged anymore.

Challenges at work are essential as they make us feel a sense of achievement, capability, and pride. When we fulfil the same tasks on a daily basis, we feel bored and unstimulated. Over time, these feelings may develop into disengagement and, in many cases, poor mental health.

Our data reveals that feeling challenged at work is one of the leading happiness factors to deteriorate over time – so this must be taken seriously.

Some workers may feel intimidated by new challenges. However, with the correct support and feedback structures, this will be less daunting for workers who suffer from confidence issues, and they too will reap the benefits of taking pride in their accomplishments.

4. People leave teams and leaders

Looking at our exit survey data it becomes clear that people leave poor teams and poor managers, not their companies. The lowest scores (the principal reasons people left the business) were 'leadership' (4.88), 'team' (3.8), and 'conflict' (2.3). This demonstrates that people, in general, are the reason that employees want to leave – this includes both management and fellow colleagues.

The data that can be gathered from why people leave a business is hugely important. It also indicates how important the alumni of your business are. My advice is to think like a university. Just because someone doesn't work for you anymore, doesn't mean they aren't part of your community and your story.

A few years ago, I attended an event at the University of Oxford and two of the big speakers were from McKinsey and Goldman Sachs. I wanted to find out why these two companies were investing so much money into their alumni networks. After a few beers in the union bar, I found out from the speakers that their alumni were part of their new business strategy. It's funny what you can find out for the cost of a couple of pints.

5. Myth busting – Blue Monday

Legend has it that the third Monday of January is the unhappiest day in the work calendar.

In the spirit of supporting awareness for wellbeing and mental health, I feel it's my duty to inform you all that according to our data, Blue Monday is a myth! I'm also aware of the dangers of self-fulfilling prophecies, so I want to do all I can to prevent this from becoming one!

Our data suggest happiness levels on Blue Monday are no different from any other Monday.

Summary: This clearly highlights that Blue Monday is a myth... there are even rumours it was created by travel companies to boost sales!

6. Female employees are unhappier at work

The data from the global workplace happiness study highlights that the gender pay gap is not the only aspect of employment female workers are unhappy with, but they are likely associated. Overall, women scored lower and therefore feel less happy at work than men. This was the case in seven of the ten factors assessed. It suggests that the gender pay gap is not the only issue in today's workplace where female employees have concerns which are either being ignored or have been allowed to persist.

'Career development opportunities' is the most serious issue with women rating their happiness at 5.8, highlighting a sense of unhappiness which needs to be addressed. Men feel they can "speak openly and honestly" more than women. This may explain why they scored a higher rating for 70% of the questions in the study; men feel more empowered to be open and honest and express their feelings without fear of repercussions.

This openness is vital to all workers' happiness and its importance cannot be underplayed.

As 60% of the responses came from women, there is clearly a lot of work to do if businesses want to reap the benefits of a happier female workforce and a stronger, overall culture.

7. There is a disconnect between what makes business owners and employees happy at work

We asked employees and business leaders from around the world what they felt were the top 10 factors affecting their happiness at work. Respondents were given a selection of 30+ factors which commonly make up the foundation of employee happiness. The 10 most popular choices were used to create The Happiness Indicator (see Figure 1), from which we established that four of the top five are shared by employers and employees alike – but the ranking of importance varies massively. Outside the top five, the disparities are even greater – the most noticeably being 'career development', which is in seventh place for employees and barely scrapes the top 20 for employers in 19th.

This marks stark differences in attitudes to the importance of these factors and shows a disconnect between employers and employees which could lead to tensions if not understood effectively. Decision-making around where to invest in people can only be effective when employers really understand their employees' needs.

Here is the table with all factors and rankings:

Factors	Employee rank	Employer rank	Difference between employee and employer rank
Feeling valued as an individual	1	3	+2
Doing a job that you enjoy	2	1	-1
Work-life balance	3	4	+1
Pay and benefits	4	9	+5
Trust in the people you work with	5	5	0
Quality of leadership	6	2	-4
Career development	7	19	+12
Ability to speak your mind openly and honestly	8	6	-2
Having control over your work (autonomy)	9	7	-2
An interesting role	10	8	-2

Figure 1: The Happiness Index Data

8. Why are engineers so unhappy?

One of the unhappiest job functions we often see in our data is engineers. Interestingly, though, in the first three months of the

Covid-19 crisis, we observed that engineers went from being one of the most unhappy professions to one of the happiest professions.

More research is needed into this area, but an early theory is that there is a relationship between unhappiness in engineers and the open plan office. Engineers seem to have been one job function that has benefited from working remotely.

9. It's time to answer the 'is bigger better?' debate

Big business can certainly learn from smaller companies when it comes to keeping employees happy. In every measure except one, SMEs were ranked higher than mid-sized and large businesses in our Happiness Indicator study. In six of the 10 questions, SMEs scored positively (7.0+), whereas that score only featured once for large companies. This aligns with the results from our Employee Net Promoter (eNPS) study which deduced that workers from smaller companies have higher eNPS scores than workers from large companies. This clearly answers the 'is bigger better?' question... with a definitive NO.

The lower scores for large companies could be explained by the lack of communication between departments resulting in workers feeling siloed and isolated. Some employees feel like they are "invisible" and that they wished they knew "how their work adds value to the business". These issues are much easier to tackle for smaller businesses.

This also goes back to the Dunbar number we discussed earlier and a reminder of why we invented The Happiness Index in the first place. As companies scale, it is harder to keep track of how employees and customers are feeling without smart use of technology.

10. Emotional deficit

One of the interesting things we observed in our data through the Covid-19 pandemic is something we have labelled emotional deficit. We found that as more workers were either remote or on furlough, their need for communication and to share their feelings increased. See Figure 2 from The Happiness Index's survey platform:

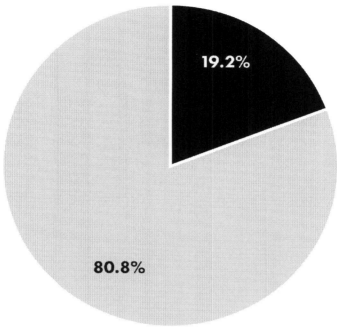

Has comment   **No comment**

Figure 2: Desire Amongst Employees to Share and Express Feelings, The Happiness Index

The pandemic has increased the desire amongst employees to share and express how they are feeling, with eight out of ten employees (80.8%) leaving comments – more than double the normal average. As well as an increase in the number of comments made, we've also seen that the comment length has more than tripled, from an average of 10 to 37 words. The amount of people feeding back has also trebled. This is an emotional deficit and a clear example of the importance of companies not pulling up the drawbridge and shutting people out.

There is a need for employers to communicate how they can

support the wellbeing of their people, with a high incidence of the data mentioning "anxiety", "stress", and "uncertainty" amongst employees.

11. Cheers, mate

Last but not least, my favourite bit of data is based on how simple and human happiness really is.

When looking at our eNPS data we get a reminder of how important recognition and feeling valued is. Verbal recognition is one of the leading happiness factors that isn't being capitalised on by many employers. The data highlights that there is an overwhelming feeling that management is not attentive enough. Staff feel like they go above and beyond but don't receive the credit.

As the old saying goes, 'please' and 'thank you' don't cost anything, but they do go a long way.

CHAPTER 14. HAPPINESS ACROSS THE GLOBE

As we discussed earlier, employee engagement is a western hangover from the post-industrial era that subconsciously views human beings as part of a machine. We focus on global happiness because, like Pixar, our research shows that better understanding of emotions gives us a deeper understanding of human behaviour.

Figure 1: Spreading Happiness Globally

Here are some of our observations from across the world.

The Irish and happiness

With a name like Matthew Phelan, perhaps it won't surprise you that although I was born in England, I am actually plastic Irish with a Brexit-busting Irish passport.

Stereotypically, the Irish are often seen as jovial people who are always up for 'the craic'. There are potential dangers with the stereotype of the Irish as constantly jolly and fun, as this can be a mask which hides potential mental health problems.

I remember growing up hearing stories of family friends in Ireland that went something like, "They just went for a walk, fell over, and died". It wasn't until I was older and understood that these were made up stories to avoid the truth that these people had taken their own lives.

On my last trip to Ireland, I met a relative of mine who had not drunk alcohol for 30 years but instead of telling people they were sober, they would just always drive to the party. Unfortunately, with many cultural stereotypes, it is easier to tell a little white lie than be a non-drinker.

And, as we know, Irish history is one that encompasses a lot of pain and struggle. Margot Slattery, Global Diversity and Inclusion Officer at Sodexo and proud Limerick fan, points out that the Irish culture, built as it is around pubs, live music, and yes, the odd drink, does facilitate and animate conversation, and brings communities together. Ultimately, relaxing and being able to use alcohol to take the edge off of shyness or social inhibitions can help you feel more like yourself and present your real and whole self to those around you, but the key – as in life – is balance.

Margot thinks that the Irish are happy people, but that it's important to see that happiness as temporary. She believes one of the things that we could learn from the Irish, when it comes to happiness, is that it's something that needs to be worked at and built upon, and certainly not be taken for granted.

One of the ways that the Irish government is currently doing this is through their work to combat racism in Ireland. As a people who were regularly discriminated against both in the UK and in the US, Margot says it's common for the Irish to feel that they can't be racist; however, this isn't the case. Ten to 12% of Ireland is now made up of those born outside of the country, and in order to help challenge the way the country is governed, particularly in respect to this growing demographic, they have created a task force to address racial justice. What Margot believes we can take away from this approach is that the Irish government are actively listening and actively participating in a dialogue around these issues.

The Danes and happiness

The Danes have taught us a lot about happiness and my personal favourite book on happiness is *The Little Book of Hygge: The Danish Way to Live Well* by Meik Wiking. Wiking is the CEO of the Happiness Research Institute in Copenhagen and has recently opened a happiness museum. Wiking says, "Hygge is the magic ingredient that makes Danes the happiest nation in the world."

Denmark is often seen as one of the happiest countries on earth. But fellow Dane Arlette Bentzen, who is a Chief Happiness Officer in Copenhagen, doesn't believe the data that Danes are actually happier than other people. She does, however, believe that Danes feel safe and protected – there's a stability there.

When you look at the questions that are asked on the surveys that pull together the data about the happiest countries, often they're not asking about your emotional happiness, but rather a wider sense of wellbeing. It's a similar problem to the employee engagement surveys.

While Danes pay higher taxes than most other countries, they have excellent social care programmes with unemployment benefits, free health care, and lots of other great resources available to them. This means that the country is quite safe – visitors are often surprised that people leave their bikes unlocked or their pushchairs and prams outside on the street when they pop into a cafe or restaurant. All of this leads to a lot of satisfaction and we discuss safety in more detail in Chapter 15: The Neuroscience of Happiness.

In Denmark they have a word that is used a lot – *arbejdsglæde* – which is actually a composite of two words: *arbejds*, meaning work, and *glæde*, meaning happiness. This is a term which is used by experts in the field but also by a lot of companies and even the Danish prime minister. The concept has been around for close to 100 years, and companies understand that if their employees are happy, are doing work that's meaningful to them, and also are around people they get along with, they do better work. This also means that when people look for jobs, they take culture and fit into account way more than perhaps we do in the UK or the US.

The key thing that we can learn from Denmark is that happiness at work isn't just important, it is expected. It's easy for management to lose sight of this. Happiness at work will increase if managers change how they manage. It's important that managers not only look at traditional KPIs but also at how happy and fulfilled their direct reports are within their job. People need to enjoy their time and feel driven and flourish at their job, and Arlette argues that this is a key part of a manager's job.

The Dutch and happiness

Although less well-known for their happiness than the Danish, my Dutch friends and colleagues insist that there's something that can be learned from the Dutch about happiness. In fact, a 2013 study by Unicef showed that Dutch children were the happiest in the world, and this year the Netherlands ranked the sixth happiest in the *World Happiness Report*, which isn't a bad score. There are lots of things this could be linked to, including lots of exercise in the form of plenty of cycling, a more measured relationship with work that leaves many feeling less stressed, good social support at a governmental level, like that discussed in Denmark, and so on.

Certainly, when I worked in marketing, there were obvious differences between our Dutch and London offices. While by 5pm our office in Utrecht, near Amsterdam, would be a ghost town, in London, most people would still be working hard until at least 6pm. Similarly, my Dutch colleagues took their lunch break very seriously, sitting together at communal tables to eat every day, with very few people skipping the break for an al desko meal. Often times, if the meal didn't last the full hour, a large group of colleagues would go on a walk around the waterways near the office to take in some fresh air. I'm told that these kinds of practices aren't uncommon in the Netherlands.

Many European countries have a similar term to *hygge*, and in Holland it's *gezellig*. The term has been much less co-opted by the interior design world, but it does have similar connotations of cosiness and comfort. The main difference is that *gezellig* is built on the word *gezel*, which finds its roots in people and their relationship to one and other. Often going down to the pub with your mates is *gezellig*, having dinner with your mum might be *gezellig*, and having a good group of colleagues around you is certainly *gezellig*. There's a sense that spaces and places are better with people who love or care for you around you.

Happiness in the US

A 2019 poll of more than 5,000 employees by Mindspace asked respondents about workplace culture. Alongside wellness and engagement, employees were asked about overall happiness. In this poll, and this was as surprising to me as I'm sure it will be to you, it was found that 93% of employees in the US were happy at work, the highest number of any country surveyed. The Netherlands came second with 91% of employees, and the UK was lowest with only 73% of employees feeling generally happy at work.

I look at this study with a very sceptical mind due to the sample size, but I do think there is some truth in linking it to job growth and opportunity. I also think companies that are likely to use Mindspace are already likely to be very forward thinking, so I suspect the employee sample is not representative.

In any country where jobs are plentiful it would likely mean that employees could choose to move to jobs where they feel more connected to the mission, their colleagues, and are able to get benefits such as health care and time off, which will help them spend more time with their friends and loved ones.

The downside of a system like this is that many people in the US lose their medical coverage if they lose their job. This seems shocking to someone from the UK where we have the NHS, but, given what we know about safety as a platform for happiness, it is no surprise that jobs are a key concern for voters in the US.

Happiness in South America

When I spoke to Pamela Teutsch Ortlieb and Rodrigo Rojas, who we work closely with at The Happiness Index, they explained to me that happiness at work has a special significance in Chile where they work.

In Chile, a country where family, relationships, and community are very important, particularly in recent times, companies have started taking on a more nurturing role within people's lives. They see that Chileans expect the organisations they work for, and their managers specifically, to take an interest in their lives, their families, and their world outside of work, and to care for them and nurture them both in and outside of the workplace.

However, they believe it's not the same in the rest of South America where there is a real north-south divide. Although there may be similarities in terms of the language spoken, and the roots of their cultures, there are significant differences throughout the region. There is a large difference between outlooks on life between Chile and their northern neighbours, even within South America, which has an impact on the way they see their working lives. They see that there's a strong connection between the weather and happiness: when there is better weather, and more sunlight, they believe that people are happier, have better relationships, and feel more relaxed.

Off on a slight weather tangent back in the UK (we Brits love our weather!), I was speaking to Noel McGonigle, the HR Director Savills UK, Europe and Middle East and he has been implementing SAD (seasonal affective disorder) awareness training amongst his employees for this reason.

Weather is one difference in Latin America, but there are also resource differences across the continent between countries that are more or less developed or are suffering political upheaval. This may not always work in the ways in which you may expect: sometimes in countries with fewer resources, be that lack of education, limited economic development, or even those with less food, these people can be the happiest. Pamela believes this is because the people in these countries understand the importance of relationships and place more of a focus on sustaining these. In order to maintain this in developed countries, Rodrigo encourages others to always make time to build and maintain relationships. This doesn't need to be complicated; in fact, simpler, he believes, is almost always better.

Happiness in Southern Africa

Africa is a huge continent, so it's important not to generalise too much; however, there is a common thread when it comes to happiness which links several neighbouring countries in the southern part of the continent. This is the idea of *ubuntu*.

Ubuntu is perhaps best known in the western world from its connection to the South African Peace and Reconciliation Committee, under Archbishop Desmond Tutu. However, this is a much older philosophy which is found across Sub-Saharan Africa, in countries such as South Africa, but also Malawi and Zimbabwe. It speaks to many aspects of community, such as sharing, respect, helpfulness, and caring for others.

In his book, *No Future Without Forgiveness*, Tutu describes *ubuntu* as follows:

> *A person with ubuntu is open and available to others, affirming of others, does not feel threatened that others are able and good, based from a proper self-assurance that comes from knowing that he or she belongs in a greater whole and is diminished when others are humiliated or diminished, when others are tortured or oppressed.*

In an interview, Nelson Mandela explained: "Ubuntu does not mean that people should not address themselves. The question therefore is: are you going to do so in order to enable the community around you to be able to improve?"

This idea of mutual support as being an important facet of community, and happiness more generally, is one that plays out in the data that we have gathered at The Happiness Index – we see time and time again that relationships with others is a key factor in why people remain in, and find happiness in, their places of work.

The Japanese and happiness

Japan has one of the oldest populations in the world, with an above average number of people reaching ages of over 100, and this is particularly evident on the island of Okinawa. Although there are undoubtedly many factors which play into their long lives (a quick Google search will return hundreds of diet pro-grammes based on what they eat claiming to help you live longer), the Okinawans themselves link their longevity to exercise, moai, and Ikigai.

As we saw in Chapter 9, exercise is scientifically linked to a number of great happiness and health benefits. *Moai* refers to the local tradition of creating supportive community groups that start in childhood and typically last for the rest of their lives. It's easy to see the parallels between this kind of community support and the *ubuntu* theology from Southern Africa. Although *moai* now refers to small friendship groups meeting with a common interest, originally *moai* referred to a community pooling together as a village to achieve a common purpose.

This sense of purpose is also important in the third reason why Okinawans live longer – *Ikigai*. Diversity and inclusion expert Kevin Withane suggests that the easiest way of translating the term *Ikigai* is to mean "the reason you get out of bed". *Ikigai* is a central tenet of traditional Japanese medicine and wellness. The reason it is linked to longevity is that when people have a firm sense of purpose and direction, they are happier and this in turn allows them to live longer.

Happiness in China

As you read in earlier chapters, overcoming the Chinese firewall has been a huge challenge for us, but working in China has been a very interesting learning curve for us all as well. When we first visited China, we were worried that our message of #FreedomToBeHuman could end with us locked up in jail. The opposite has been true, and we have been welcomed by the people of China and companies of China.

Just discussing China in the West is controversial, and I am deeply concerned when I read stories like the following on the BBC:

> *China is accused of locking up hundreds of thousands of Muslims without trial in its western region of Xinjiang.*

> *The government denies the claims, saying people willingly attend special "vocational schools" which combat "terrorism and religious extremism".*

But I want to offer you my balanced view. To not include both sides of my Chinese experience would mean not being 100% honest with you, the reader. China is a paradox in many ways. Despite all it is criticised for, it is also a leader in areas like green tech and setting global green targets. Take for example its pledge to be carbon neutral before 2060. It also leads the world in female business ownership and entrepreneurship.

An interesting fact I found out when in China is that the symbol of HR is 人事. The direct translation of that is not 'human resources' but 'people matter'. I know which one I prefer. HR rebrand, anyone?

In our platform, we consistently see Chinese employees amongst the happiest in the world. In a recent Happiness Index global study of 185,000+ employees worldwide, we found that Chinese employees scored a table topping eNPS score 52.6 vs the global average of 39.3.

In the same study we can also see that Chinese employees are the most optimistic about the future. This is the data, but this was also observed by our Head of Robots, Matt Stannard, on his last trip to China: "The one thing I took from my time in China is the optimism of the everyday employee." And that means a lot considering Matt's background as an Ipswich Town Football Club season ticket holder, a group of fans not exactly known for their optimism.

Happiness in Australian cities

The world is urbanising. At time of writing, 4.2 billion people, more than half the world's population, live in cities, with this number set to increase to more than six billion by 2045. The *World Happiness Report* suggests that by 2050, seven in 10 people worldwide will be city dwellers. With all this urbanisation, there are certain challenges to happiness. High housing costs, lack of public infrastructure and increased pollution have an effect on happiness.

Australia, despite the outback depiction many people have of the country, actually has the highest percentage of its population living in urban environments. The *World Happiness Report* has found that a large number of these cities are in the top 20 happiest in the world: Brisbane is number 10, while Melbourne and Perth sit at 13 and 14, and Sydney is the 20th happiest city in the world. In fact, Australia has more cities in the top 20 than any other country. Obviously, it's a bit bigger than Denmark or New Zealand, who have two and three cities in the top 20 respectively, but there's a lot we can learn from Australian cities.

Australians cite their café culture, smaller city sizes, and laid-back outlook on life as reasons as to why their cities are particularly happy. The *World Happiness Report* itself gives several factors in city-wide happiness: reduced commuting times, air pollution, and access to green and public open spaces (Don't forget they have awesome city beaches). This would certainly be an interesting area for more research for the future, and I'm looking forward to seeing what makes Australian cities such a great place to live.

Happiness in Antarctica

Just to prove happiness really is a global phenomenon, I wanted to point out an interesting study out of Antarctica, where NASA has been studying team dynamics to help them with the happiness of crews travelling to Mars (soon happiness will be studied on other planets!). Because Antarctica is such an extreme environment and teams there are unable to leave the continent for months at a time, there are a couple of studies investigating team dynamics and happiness in a remote location.

One of the main findings uncovered by scientists researching these teams is that the "social relationships people form is an important predictor to how well they can complete tasks together", according to Leslie DeChurch, PhD. An important part of this is humour. Certainly, astronauts have already reported the way that humour is key for diffusing tense situations. Research has also demonstrated the 'clown role' in team dynamics.

Teams in Antarctica have also shown the importance of bonding and light relief. Whether it's going out and celebrating good weather conditions with a silly dance or encouraging 'in jokes' that help break up the monotony of a long winter, these kinds of moments encourage interactions between the team members and mean that everyone gets along better.

Happiness in the UK

It may surprise my fellow UK residents, but as Meik Wiking pointed out in our *Happiness and Humans* podcast interview, the Danes look to the UK with envy in one important area which is data.

The Office for National Statistics (ONS) has started including four wellbeing questions in their national surveys on what they call Measuring National Wellbeing. Significantly, one of the four questions is focused on national happiness. Here are the questions:

1) Overall, how satisfied are you with your life nowadays?

2) Overall, to what extent do you feel that the things you do in your life are worthwhile?
3) Overall, how happy did you feel yesterday?
4) Overall, how anxious did you feel yesterday?

Summary

The Happiness Index is now collecting independent anonymous data from employees in over 90 countries. Every single country in the world when viewed from the outside has big issues, and we often discuss the moral dilemmas of working in all these countries, BUT we always conclude (perhaps arrogantly) that the country is better off by giving employees an independent voice and offering what we call: #FreedomToBeHuman.

CHAPTER 15. THE NEUROSCIENCE OF HAPPINESS

At The Happiness Index, we started using the knowledge and understanding from neuroscience in 2017, but it wasn't until late 2019 when we started to link neuroscience research and happiness into the way we work and the way we build out technology.

For example, a lot of survey technology tries to engage with people first before a company has proven it: a) cares, and b) listens. If you try to engage with any human being in a meaningful way before you have proved that you care and you are listening, you are only going to scratch the surface. This is one of the reasons why so many technology transformation projects fail.

Emotions at work

Emotions have been pushed out of organisations for too long. Just one example of how important emotions are is the research that associates emotions with memory.

The 2017 paper, "The Influences of Emotion on Learning and Memory" by Tyng, Amin, Saad, and Malik, concludes: "Substantial evidence has established that emotional events are remembered more clearly, accurately and for longer periods of time than are neutral events."

Emotions allow us to recall events in a more meaningful way. Banning emotions from the workplace is hurting not only individuals but a company's ability to perform and in turn financial results. It is time to stop labelling people 'too emotional'.

The same paper goes on to say:

Emotion has a substantial influence on the cognitive pro-cesses in humans, including perception, attention, learning, memory, reasoning, and problem solving. Emotion has a par-ticularly strong influence on attention, especially modulating the selectivity of attention as well as motivating action and behavior.

If there was a magic spell that you could buy that would im-prove perception, attention, learning, memory, reasoning, and problem solving, you would. Luckily, all you need to do is let emotions like happiness back into your organisations. For too long employee engagement programmes have been keeping the door shut. The more real time data we collect, the more we see the importance of aligning employee engagement with em-ployee happiness.

Figure 1: The Happiness Index: Reconnecting the Heart and the Brain

Happiness is an emotion and a feeling. It speaks to the heart and provides energy. Engagement is purpose and clarity – it speaks to the brain and provides direction. Both are important but one shouldn't be more important than the other.

As Mr Miyagi said in the *Karate Kid*, "The lesson is not just for karate only. The lesson is for the whole life. If your whole life has balance, everything will be better."

The data and neuroscience is telling us we could quite easily replace the word karate with the word HR in this quote if we wanted to humanise employee engagement.

The calm down test (don't do this test)

The easy way to mimic the traditional employee engagement process where emotional feeling and rational thinking are out of balance is the 'calm down test'. The next time you see someone visibly stressed at work ask them to 'calm down'. I would bet that in the entire known record of human existence that nobody has calmed down based on the instruction of another person asking them to. In fact, you will probably find the person becomes more stressed.

THIS is what happens when a company who treats you badly doesn't listen and gives you no voice, BUT then suddenly asks you to fill out a 50-question annual employee engagement survey. This is why so many companies message me saying their employee engagement scores are reaching record high levels, but people are leaving, productivity is down, and burnout is high.

To go deeper and to understand your people, you really need to invest time first in showing you care and that you want to listen. We also found from combining neuroscience and happiness data that emotions are a much quicker way to understand people.

Emotions as a data point

For too long, emotions have been ignored and actively discouraged at work. I have definitely been labelled as 'too emotional', but our neuroscientists tell us that scientifically there is actually no such thing. So, the next time someone tells you that you are too emotional, perhaps ask them for the science behind their comment.

Tennis coach Patrick Mouratoglou in the Netlfix documentary, *The Playbook*, was reflecting on mistakes he had made in his career when he said he "let his emotions make decisions". For me, the balance is listening to your emotions, taking in advice, and reading the data available and then making a decision. Yes, an emotion shouldn't make a business decision as Patrick points out, but it shouldn't be ignored.

Somewhere along the line, businesspeople have blocked out the first stage of listening to your emotions for fear of letting your emotions make decisions. These days I simply see my emotions as another data source to chuck into the mix. For me, as a data geek, to ignore emotions would be to ignore a very rich source of data.

Safety

Clive Hyland, our Head of Neuroscience at The Happiness Index, states once we feel safe and content, then we can engage. Engagement is a brain state which can be built on top of the heart state of contentment.

Clive argues that by linking happiness to performance, then the HR team can move forward with the CEO and c-suite on a path that is completely scientifically based.

According to him, the science backs up the intuition, whereby we shouldn't be forcing people to fit within an organisation, but rather should be finding talented committed people and building a light organisation which fits around them. This allows your talent to flourish and grow and makes them want to be there. The traditional way of working, where we force people to perform, doesn't work. He argues that giving people the room and space to learn and grow and will lead to far greater performance levels.

What is neuroscience?

It's easy to be put off by the word science. Some see science as hard or boring, and certainly many of our politicians would like us to believe that science isn't really relevant to the real world.

However, if you can get beyond your initial feelings, or any left-over resentment from your school days, there's a lot to be gained from looking into neuroscience. It's amazing if you remove the anxiety of exams, how fun science can be.

In the last century, psychology took us a long way in our understanding of humans, the brain, and the way we all function. However, in my opinion, since the turn of the century, this has plateaued a bit. But now advances in neuroscience are allowing us to discover more about how the mind and body works together.

Neuroscience allows us to look at brains in operation – we're no longer confined to making theories from the outside. We can look at what's actually going on in the brain; of course, we are pretty early on in the journey, but we have already started to understand more about the brain and the nervous system.

Neuroscience helps psychology feel less abstract. All of us are working with human brains every single day, not only the human brains of our colleagues and clients, but also our own. There's always more to find out about human nature, including yourself.

People often find themselves asking questions which are intrinsically linked to neuroscience. Why did I react like that? Why am I not happier with my life? Why do I always end up in these kinds of situations?

Personally, the more neuroscience research I read and study, the more I feel I can connect and better understand my friends, colleagues, and family.

What can neuroscience teach us about happiness?

As we see in Figure 2, our instinctive, emotional, reflective, and rational parts of the brain are all part of one beautiful ecosystem.

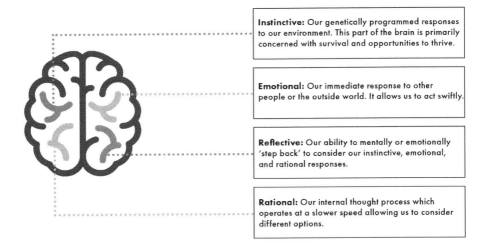

Instinctive: Our genetically programmed responses to our environment. This part of the brain is primarily concerned with survival and opportunities to thrive.

Emotional: Our immediate response to other people or the outside world. It allows us to act swiftly.

Reflective: Our ability to mentally or emotionally 'step back' to consider our instinctive, emotional, and rational responses.

Rational: Our internal thought process which operates at a slower speed allowing us to consider different options.

Figure 2: The Neuroscience of Happiness from The Happiness Index

Happiness is an emotion, and emotions are sensations in the body which are sent to the brain in order to allow the brain to do something. Emotions themselves are an expression of our instincts. When we take it down to the instinctive level, happiness is when we intuitively sense an opportunity to grow: when we feel an opportunity to be ourselves, to be honest, to put ourselves out there, when we feel safe and can express ourselves – in short, when we fulfil who we are capable of being.

We also know that there are different levels of happiness. There are transient moments of joy, but there is also a deeper and more ongoing type of happiness that we might call contentment. This is not about the temporary peaks we have when we're having fun, but rather it's about the basic feeling we carry with us. This lays the foundation for our resilience going forward. So, this contentment side of happiness is ultimately about feeling safe. When we feel safe, the hormonal balance in the brain changes, and hormones come in which allow us to engage.

Safety is the foundation of Maslow's famous hierarchy of needs but also the foundation of performance at work. Once you start thinking about safety as the platform for performance, you

suddenly start questioning why people take 12 months to hire someone and then put them on probation. Think about the word probation and ask yourself if that is one of the first experiences you want your employees to go through. Does someone being on probation give them the best platform to perform? I would encourage you to look through your entire
organisational structure and ask this one simple question: does this give our employees the best platform to perform? You can ask it of every process and system within your organisation.

What can neuroscience teach us about employee engagement?

Once you feel happy and safe, you're able to act on the happiness that you have. People are able to use the energetic commitment they have. This is how we get to meaning. In this way, happiness is a heart state and meaning is a brain or mind state.

The engagement process is all about showing people the inspiring journey you have to offer, so that people can begin to imagine themselves as part of that process, which allows for the expression of a thrive instinct. It's this thrive instinct that is translated into the emotion we call happiness.

We built the happiness and engagement model (Figure 3) to humanise employee engagement. We have also moved away from using the term high performance and replaced it with Thriving culture. High performance can have negative connotations related to mental health and can easily morph into a competitive environment. Please use this model to plot your organisation in the four-box quadrant.

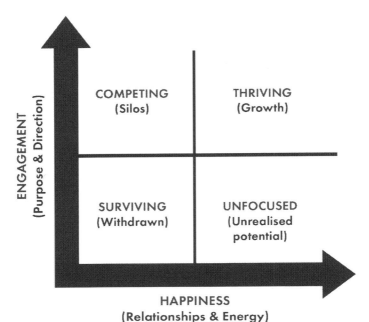

Figure 3: Happiness and Engagement Model

What else can neuroscience teach us about the link between happiness and performance?

Neuroscience can begin to explain the mechanics of how happiness aligns with performance. Until now, we've been operating on the assumption that people should be moulded to fit the organisation. What we believe at The Happiness Index, and this is underpinned by science, is that it should actually be the other way around. We should be finding talented, committed people, and building light organisations to support them. We all know that when we're around these kinds of really inspiring people we feel that buzz and we want to get out there and do it. Performance is built into us.

This links back again to the thrive instinct – we want to get that feedback from society that we're doing well and the acknowledgement from our organisation that we're performing.

The platform for performance is emotional. For far too long we've focused on the rational and practical: on systems, processes, and legislation. This is because fundamentally we've operated on a system with a lack of trust – that if you don't control people they will not perform. But this is actually rubbish; people have been performing in spite of these structures, not because of them. If you give the right person an environment to perform, the opportunity to perform, appreciate them, acknowledge them, and they will perform.

Here are some examples of how we have collected data and then used our understanding of behaviour to turn it into insight and then action.

Data

In a Happiness Index data sample of 240,000+ respondents, one of the most important factors in achieving high employee happiness is that the employee receives regular feedback from their manager.

Insight

Humans are not well programmed to receive or give feedback. Our bodies are constantly scanning for threats in the environment. If we feel under attack, the body will not send the correct nutrients to the brain such as oxygen. Feedback in a poor culture can be perceived as a threat by the body and starve the brain of the nutrients it needs to perform.

Action

Build a feedback culture where everyone in the company feels comfortable giving and receiving feedback. Simple training can help create a culture where individuals seek out feedback and thrive.

Data

Nearly 20% of US workers experience bullying in the workplace and 19% witness it. According to a national survey conducted by the Workplace Bullying Institute (WBI), 60.4 million Americans are affected by bullying.

Insight

Unlike physical pain, emotional pain triggered by workplace stress is spread throughout the body, and we therefore expend energy trying to locate the problem.

Action

Create a listening culture where all employees from all backgrounds and seniority levels have a voice. Bullying thrives in a culture of secrecy where only the few feel able to speak up. The energy wasted by bullying can be re-channelled towards achieving the vision of the organisation.

CHAPTER 16. INTRODUCING THE QUANTUM WAY

So, if we replace a traditional command and control approach, what are we going to replace it with? Will it be anarchy? Will our staff just be wandering around in the woods playing with dirt and doing no work?

The quantum way

I believe in something that we have been evolving over the last six years that we recently named the quantum way. The approach and idea was introduced to us by Clive Hyland, and, in his words, we have taken the concept and run with it. Huge, huge credit must go to our leadership team with special mention to Jackie Dyal and Gemma Shambler for championing it and Tony Latter for being the custodian of the Quantum way so we can share it with you.

Energetic beings

We have used a lot of real time data, neuroscience, and quantum physics to build this idea. The central core concept is that we are all energetic beings.

Quantum organisations are people-centric and built on talent and collaboration. The structure is light and flexible to create agility and autonomy. It's not about hierarchies and command and control management styles, which tend to put people into boxes.

In quantum organisations, the boxes disappear. It's about the belief that people will connect with a cause, and, if they are sufficiently committed and adequately supported, they will become self-organising. The organisation becomes organic and the need for hierarchies and structure is removed. The key for organisations is to identify what the common cause is so it can inspire their people, and they can then channel their energy towards it and connect with it.

Fields of meaning

By grouping communities or teams around a cause, they become connected to each other and they reach a state of flow, created by an energetic connection. As humans, we are drawn towards these energetic connections and in physics they call it 'fields of meaning'.

When teams create these connections, they no longer need to be accountable to line managers. There still needs to be ways of supporting and overseeing performance, which can be achieved through mentoring, but what you're relying on is the team's desire to perform in their own right. Achieving because they want to and not because they have to. In the past, a performance issue was the manager's issue; now it's the team's issue. It needs to be addressed in a different way, but once addressed the outcome is far more powerful.

Symbiotic system

One of the major issues with traditional structures is that when people are no longer suited to an organisation, they are often managed out or leave. It shouldn't be like that. Organisations need to recognise where that person's passion is at that point in time and focus that passion on a new cause. This creates a situation where the individual and the organisation can grow in parallel.

Every day we are dealing with a dynamic environment which we need to respond to. Therefore, the talent needs of an organisation are going to change over time. So, we have to let go of the structured past and let something new in. This is a big step, and it's about believing in people.

Energy

The whole concept of quantum organisations is about a connection to a cause, and this means you'll start off with a team who is channeling their energy and enthusiasm towards the cause. However, as time goes by, those teams will need to be fluid and refreshed as people's energy and enthusiasm wanes.

Vision as an energy source

Rather than a top-down hierarchy attempting to control energy, everything will gravitate towards a vision that is used to unite people internally and externally. It is really important to define your vision and values before dismantling a hierarchical structure, or chaos will prevail.

We use the solar system as a simple visualisation because the energy comes from the sun see Figure 1) that fuels the planets (the causes). Ultimately, this replaces departmental structures like sales and marketing with for example growth and brand. The overall goal of this system is to remove a silo mentality that sucks in energy and replaces it with a system where the entire company is pulled in one direction. The role of the leadership is to become the custodian of the vision and nurturer of the values.

Figure 1: The Quantum Way from The Happiness Index

Guidelines not rules

For quantum organisations to work, there needs to be a set of guiding principles. These are not structured rules, but they give individuals an understanding of how a quantum organisation works. Removing large traditional command and control structures can be scary, and organisations do need some kind of guidelines to help support employees. The key word here is support. Here are the nine guiding principles of quantum organisations; we call them the 'Quantum 9' (see Figure 2).

What is the approach?

1. Light touch

Teams need to be agile, flexible, and evolve over time as people's energy and enthusiasm levels change. Teams are able to focus on delivering a high-quality outcome quickly because they have the autonomy to make decisions.

2. Embedded learning

Individuals will have the opportunities to grow and develop as they are exposed to situations that require them to use their skills and knowledge to make decisions. It's important individuals embed this knowledge to help them grow and have a greater impact.

3. Self-organising

Over time, teams become self-organising, which creates fluidity in the way they work and the makeup of the team. It removes the constraints of a traditional hierarchical structure.

How does it work culturally?

4. Trust

By having a team of people who are connected to a common cause trust starts to develop. This trust is both in the individual themselves and their colleagues. It links to one of the foundations of a quantum organisation, which is to always assume positive intent.

5. Ownership and accountability

By promoting autonomy, individuals need to proactively take ownership and accountability of their work. They need to be outcome focused and comfortable with taking responsibility for making their own decisions.

6. Personal growth and meaning

The neuroscience of happiness has shown us that happiness leads to personal growth and meaning. This will flow from the individual into the organisation. It creates a connection between ourselves and our work.

How will we achieve alignment across the organisation?

7. Self-aware

With the removal of a traditional line manager, individuals need to become used to giving and receiving feedback. It's this feedback which allows the individual to self-analyse the impact their contribution is having.

8. Diverse
When creating teams, it's important to embrace diversity. Teams with greater diversity tend to be more comfortable with embracing different ways of working, thinking, and feeling. They are more creative and innovative, and these are important skills to a quantum organisation.

9. Collaborative
By creating teams of people who are connected to the same cause, there is a natural collaboration. It stops teams from working in silos.

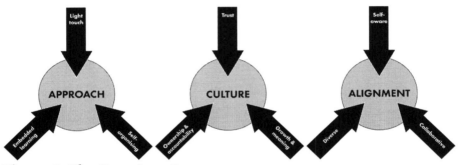

Figure 2: The Quantum 9

So, how is a quantum organisation different from the hierarchical model?
Fundamentally, it comes down to giving the individual more autonomy and ownership. Rather than having a management structure and parental relationships with the organisation, individuals are mentored and coached to equip them with the skill and experiences they need to excel in their roles. Management-led decisions and escalations are replaced with empowerment and proactive problem solving.

The benefits of a quantum organisation are a more creative, empowered, and productive workforce – all of which build shareholder value. It shows that investing in your people and giving them the opportunities to develop new skills – and empowering them to use them – improves your company's performance.

The primary benefit for individuals is happiness. Empowerment to make decisions gives us autonomy, while connecting to a common cause provides us with a purpose, and embedding learning of new skills and experiences gives us a sense of growth and progress. All of these play a fundamental role in an individual's happiness at work.

Is the quantum way new?
Have a look around you and you will see brands that are already working in a quantum way naturally. Use the above list and see how many points your company is scoring or, for a bit of benchmarking, run the list against companies you admire. From B Corps to the Zebras not Unicorns movement, we are seeing a shift to what we call quantum working.

Compromise sucks
Nobody likes to compromise and I for one don't want to choose between the environment, my family, and my livelihood. The latest science and data is showing us that we don't need to. The global pandemic has given us all a wake up call that the world of work we have built isn't working.

The way forward
Quantum working gives us a way of balancing all parts of our life to achieve success at home, in our communities, through our work and for our planet. With the right combination of human emotion, rational thinking, technology, and good old-fashioned human ingenuity, we can build a better way.

Quantum working is simply a set of principles encouraging us to work in a more natural way suited to human beings – a way in which organisations can thrive and GROW symbiotically with their people.

CHAPTER 17. FREEDOM TO BE HAPPY: THE BUSINESS CASE FOR HAPPINESS

So, I have taken you almost as far as I can. I can't actually write your business case for you, BUT I can help you in a quantum way. Ninety percent of the job is truly believing there is a better way of doing things.

I hope this book has backed up what you already knew. The fact you picked up this book means you already suspect that happiness is important; you probably just needed a bit of encouragement and data from me to pursue what you already knew in your gut.

If you really believe in this stuff and back yourself, you will be surprised how many people are prepared to listen, but you will need to go to people prepared. You need a business case for happiness that is unique to you and your business.

The happiness revolution

As Benjamin Franklin of "the pursuit of happiness" fame may or may not have said, "By failing to prepare, you are preparing to fail".

We know that all good business cases are a combination of data, evidence, and storytelling. And preparation!

Seven

You are about to roll your dice on your happiness revolution. My last bit of data for you is that if you were to roll two dice, seven is the most likely outcome to occur.

So, to give your one-person revolution a chance of succeeding, here are my seven top tips for making a business case for happiness.

1. Audience

Think hard about your audience for this business case and apply a weighting to the plan. For example, if someone is a numbers person, weight the quantity of the plan to 70% evidence / 10% story / 20% case studies.

2. Adapt

Consider what is important to your audience. For example, if your audience is passionate about wellbeing, then use the Jeremy Dawson data. If they want real time data, use some of the bits from The Happiness Index data. If they are big on productivity, use the Jan-Emmanuel De Neve evidence.

3. Test

Show the plan to a wide range of people and ask for honest feedback. To make it easy on the person you are asking I suggest wording it as such: **"How can I improve this plan?"**

That way your polite friends are invited to be honest and not just be nice to protect your feelings. Polite friends are not helping prepare the CEO for the shareholders who are going to challenge this plan. Approach your most brutal friends and colleagues – you know who they are.

If you can't explain your plan to the normal person in the street, you haven't got the storytelling bit right. Recruit people who don't know your business or sector and road test the plan on them.

Remember the bit in my *Happiness and Humans* podcast interview with Alex Edmans where he explains that the happiness of employees flows through to financial results regardless of the industry? Obvious when you think about it, but good to have this study in your back pocket if you are told, 'this industry doesn't work like that'. Twenty-eight years of data should be enough to get their attention.

4. Measurement

Consider how you will measure the change you wish to create. Think of Peter Drucker. If Drucker was reading this, he would probably be thinking about some SMART objectives to make sure this plan is robust.

The SMART acronym stands for specific, measurable, attainable, relevant, and time-bound.

5. Concise

If you can't fit this plan on one page, then you don't have a plan.

6. Back yourself

Only present a business plan you truly believe in. If you are having last minute doubts about sharing your happiness revolution, just watch Hamilton the musical.

7. Last chance saloon

If all else fails, there is always one last argument…

Creating a workplace with happy employees is way better for your own happiness. Who wants to work in an environment where people are unhappy anyway?

As Lara Aknin pointed out in her research, giving can increase your own happiness. It turns out giving others happiness is the most beautifully selfish thing you can do.

So, go forth you SELFISH, selfish human being and make people happy… very happy. You might even reduce mortality rates, increase productivity, and make a serious load of dosh along the way…

Cheers,

Matt, The Business Case For Happiness :-)

CHAPTER 18. THE HAPPINESS AND HUMANS COMMUNITY

I hope you enjoyed my first – and possibly last – book.

If you want to continue your journey with people committed to a more positive future of work, please join our Happiness and Humans Community.

Community

Join The Happiness and Humans Global Community here:
tinyurl.com/joinhappyhumans

Podcast

Listen to many of the experts featured in this book on the *Happiness and Humans* Podcast:
tinyurl.com/HappinessAndHumans

Connect with me

Connect with me on LinkedIn:
https://www.linkedin.com/in/matthewphelan/

Follow me on Twitter

https://twitter.com/MatthewPhelan

Visualise your culture

If you have enjoyed the data and insight in this book and would like to visualise the culture of your organisation, please scan the QR code below to book a demo of The Happiness Index.

BIBLIOGRAPHY

Chapter 1. Why Happiness?

Lyubomirsky, Sonja and Laura King. "The Benefits of Frequent Positive Affect: Does Happiness Lead to Success?" *Psychological Bulletin*, vol. 131, no. 6 (2005): 803–855. https://www.apa.org/pubs/journals/releases/bul-1316803.pdf.

Chapter 2. What is Happiness?

What is happiness to me?

Harari, Yuval Noah. "Were we happier in the stone age?" Guardian, September 5, 2014. https://www.theguardian.com/books/2014/sep/05/were-we-happier-in-the-stone-age.

Harari, Yuval Noah. Sapiens: A Brief History of Humankind. New York: Vintage, 2015.

Confucius

Selwood, Dominic. "On this day in 551 BC: Confucius, creator of the Chinese approach to living, is born." *Telegraph*, September 28, 2017. https://www.telegraph.co.uk/news/2017/09/28/day-551-bc-confucius-creator-chinese-approach-living-born/.

Schuman, Michael A. *Confucius: And the World He Created*. New York: Basic Books, 2015.

Chin, Annping. "Confucius." *Encyclopædia Britannica*, last modified October 19, 2020. https://www.britannica.com/biography/Confucius.

Luo, Shirong. *Happiness and the Good Life: A Classical Confucian Perspective*. Dao, 18, (2019): 41–58. https://doi.org/10.1007/

s11712-018-9640-8.

Chang, Lily. "Aristotle on Happiness: A Comparison with Confucius." PhD diss., University of Missouri – Columbia, 2006. https://mospace.umsystem.edu/xmlui/bitstream/handle/10355/4335/research.pdf?sequence=3&isAllowed=y.

Weiming, Tu. "The *Analects* as the embodiment of Confucian ideas." *Encyclopædia Britannica*, accessed October 21, 2020. https://www.britannica.com/topic/Confucianism.

Aristotle

Kenny, Anthony J.P., and Anselm H. Amadio. "Aristotle." *Encyclopædia Britannica*. March 30, 2020. https://www.britannica.com/biography/Aristotle.

Aristotle, *Nicomachean Ethics*. Edited by J.A.K. Thomson and Hugh Treddenick. London: Penguin Classics, 2004.

Aristotle, *The Politics*. Edited by Trevor Saunders. London: Penguin Classics, 2000.

Guthrie, W.K.C. *A History of Greek Philosophy, Vol. 6*. Cambridge: Cambridge University Press, 1990.

Hughes, Gerald J. *Routledge Philosophy Guidebook to Aristotle on Ethics*. London: Routledge, 2001.

The Stoics

Sellers, John. "Want to be happy? Then live like a Stoic for a week." The Conversation, September 28, 2018. https://theconversation.com/want-to-be-happy-then-live-like-a-stoic-for-a-week-103117.

Salzgeber, Jonas. *The Little Book of Stoicism: Timeless Wisdom to Gain Resilience, Confidence, and Calmness*. 2019.

Epictetus. *The Enchiridion*. Translated by Elizabeth Carter. The Internet Classics Archive, accessed October 21, 2020. http://classics.mit.edu/Epictetus/epicench.html.

Freud

Jay, Martin Evan. "Sigmund Freud." *Encyclopædia Britannica,* last modified September 19, 2020. https://www.britannica.com/biography/Sigmund-Freud.

Kringelbach, Morten L. and Kent C. Berridge. "The Neuroscience of Happiness and Pleasure." *Soc Res* (New York). 2010 SUMMER; 77(2): 659–678. https://www.ncbi.nlm.nih.gov/pmc/articles/PMC3008658/.

Loptson, Peter. *Readings on Human Nature.* Petersborough: Broadview Press, 1997.

Freud, Sigmund. *Civilisation and Its Discontents.* Translated by David McLintock. London: Penguin Classics, 2002.

Ralls, Emily and Caroline Riggs. *The Little Book of Psychology.* Chichester: Summersdale, 2019.

Positive psychology

Cherry, Kendra. "Martin Seligman Biography: The Father of Modern Positive Psychology." *Verywell Mind,* March 27, 2020. https://www.verywellmind.com/martin-seligman-biography-2795527.

Positive Psychology Centre, University of Pennsylvania. https://ppc.sas.upenn.edu.

"Eudaemonia, The Good Life: A Talk with Martin Seligman." Edge. March 23, 2004. http://www.edge.org/3rd_culture/seligman04/seligman_index.html.

Authentic Happiness, University of Pennsylvania. https://www.authentichappiness.sas.upenn.edu.

Seligman, Martin. "The new era of positive psychology." TED, February 2004. https://www.ted.com/talks/martin_seligman_the_new_era_of_positive_psychology.

Seligman, Martin E.P. *Learned Optimism: How to Change Your Mind and Your Life.* New York: Vintage, 2006.

Cherry, Kendra. "The Field of Positive Psychology." *Verywell Mind*, May 15, 2020. https://www.verywellmind.com/what-is-positive-psychology-2794902.

Chapter 3. Can Money Make You Happy?

Can having money make me happy?

Lyubomirsky, Sonya. *The Myths of Happiness*. New York: Penguin Random House, 2013.

Diener, Ed and Shigehiro Oishi. "Money and Happiness: Income and Subjective Well-being across Nations." In *Culture and Subjective Well-Being,* ed. Ed Diener and Eunkook M. Suh. Cambridge, MA: MIT Press, 2000.

Lyubomirsky, Sonya. "Does Money Really Buy Happiness?" *Psychology Today*, September 29, 2014. https://www.psychologytoday.com/gb/blog/how-happiness/201409/does-money-really-buy-happiness.

Donnelly, Grant E., Tianyi Zheng, Emily Haisley, and Michael I. Norton. "The Amount and Source of Millionaires' Wealth (Moderately) Predicts Their Happiness." https://www.hbs.edu/faculty/Publication%20Files/donnelly%20zheng%20haisley%20norton_26bec744-c924-4a28-8439-5a74abe9c8da.pdf.

Luscombe, Belinda. "Do We Need $75,000 a Year to Be Happy?" *Time*, September 6, 2010. http://content.time.com/time/magazine/article/0,9171,2019628,00.html.

Kahneman, Daniel, and Angus Deaton. "High income improves evaluation of life but not emotional well-being." *Proceedings of the National Academy of Sciences of the United States of America*, August 4, 2010. https://www.princeton.edu/~deaton/downloads/deaton_kahneman_high_income_improves_evaluation_August2010.pdf.

Donnelly, Grant E., Tianyi Zheng, Emily Haisley, and Michael I. Norton. "The Amount and Source of Millionaires' Wealth (Moderately) Predicts Their Happiness." https://

www.researchgate.net/
publication/322433835_The_Amount_and_Source_of_Million-
aires'_Wealth_Moderately_Predict_Their_Happiness.

Nadin, Gethin. *A World of Good: Lessons from Around the World in Improving the Employee Experience*. CreateSpace Independent Publishing Platform, 2017.

Nadin, Gethin. "Can money make you happy with Gethin Nadin." *Happiness and Humans*, September 1, 2020. https://open.spotify.com/episode/5FkfmXOOE2MEMKCWWsj3b4.

Can spending money make you happy?

Gilovich, Thomas, Amit Kumar, and Lily Jampol. "A wonderful life: experiential consumption and the pursuit of happiness." *Journal of Consumer Psychology* (September 2014). https://onlinelibrary.wiley.com/doi/abs/10.1016/j.jcps.2014.08.004.

Dunn, Elizabeth, Lara Aknin, Michael Norton. "Spending Money on Others Promotes Happiness." *Science* 319, 5870 (April 2008): 1687–8. https://www.researchgate.net/publication/5494996_Spending_Money_on_Others_Promotes_Happiness.

Dunn, Elizabeth W., Lara B. Aknin, Michael I. Norton. "Prosocial Spending and Happiness: Using Money to Benefit Others Pays Off." *Current Directions in Psychological Science*, vol. 23, 1 (February 2014): 41–47. https://journals.sagepub.com/doi/full/10.1177/0963721413512503.

Dunn, Elizabeth. "Helping others makes us happier – but it matters how we do it." TED, April 2019. https://www.ted.com/talks/elizabeth_dunn_helping_others_makes_us_happier_but_it_matters_how_we_do_it?language=en.

Dunn, Elizabeth. "Happiness and Money." Pop! Tech, January 3, 2011. https://www.youtube.com/watch?v=bwmWHV79vTQ.

Lyubomirsky, Sonja. "How To Buy Happiness: What Good Is Money If It Can't Buy Happiness?" *Psychology Today*, September

2, 2013. https://www.psychologytoday.com/us/blog/how-happiness/201309/how-buy-happiness.

"Planning & Progress Study 2018." Northwestern Mutual. https://news.northwesternmutual.com/planning-and-progress-2018.

"25 million UK employees affected by money worries while at work." Close Brothers Asset Management. https://www.closebrothersam.com/for-employers/news-and-insights/25-million-uk-employees-affected-by-money-worries-while-at-work/.

Kahneman, Daniel, and Angus Deaton. "High income improves evaluation of life but not emotional well-being." *Proceedings of the National Academy of Sciences of the United States of America*, August 4, 2010. https://www.princeton.edu/~deaton/downloads/deaton_kahneman_high_income_improves_evaluation_August2010.pdf.

Chapter 4. Is Happiness Nature or Nurture?

Lyubomirsky, Sonya. *The Myths of Happiness*. New York: Penguin Random House, 2013.

Lyubomirsky, Sonya. "What Determines Happiness?" Greater Good Science Centre, July 8, 2010. https://www.youtube.com/watch?v=_URP3-V1sY4.

Lyubomirsky, Sonya. "The How of Happiness with Sonja Lyubomirsky, PhD, at Happiness and Its Causes 2016." Happy & Well, March 22, 2018. https://www.youtube.com/watch?v=F7JDbP_x8So&t=1378s.

The first 50%: genetics

De Neve, Jan-Emmanuel, Nicholas A. Christakis, James H. Fowler, and Bruno S. Frey. "Genes, Economics, and Happiness." CESifo Working Paper Series, no. 2946 (August 2012). Available at SSRN: https://ssrn.com/abstract=1553633.

Etcoff, Nancy. "Set Point Match: Studies of Identical Twins

Suggest the Blueprint for Joy Is in Our Genes. Yet Brain Images Show Our Happiness Levels Can Change According to Circumstance, Activities, and Patterns of Thought. Is the Pursuit of Positive Emotions a Mixed-Up Game of Nature and Nurture?" *Science & Spirit*, vol. 17, no. 2 (March–April 2006). https://www.questia.com/magazine/1G1-171141171/set-point-match-studies-of-identical-twins-suggest.

Haworth, C.M.A., S.K. Nelson., K. Layous, K. Carter, K. Jacobs Bao, S. Lyubomirsky, et al. (2016) "Stability and Change in Genetic and Environmental Influences on Well-Being in Response to an Intervention." *PloS one*, 11, 5 (2016). http://sonjalyubomirsky.com/files/2012/09/Haworth-et-al.-2016.pdf.

The 10%: environment

Lyubomirsky, Sonya. *The Myths of Happiness*. New York: Penguin Random House, 2013.

Sonja Lyubomirsky, *The How of Happiness: A Scientific Approach to Getting the Life You Want*. New York: Penguin Random House, 2008.

Lucas, Richard E., Andrew E. Clark, Yannis Georgellis, and Ed Diener. "Reexamining Adaptation and the Set Point Model of Happiness: Reactions to Changes in Marital Status." *Journal of Personality and Social Psychology*, vol. 84, no. 3, (2003): 527–539. https://static1.squarespace.com/static/54694fa6e4b0eaec4530f99d/t/54c7048ee4b0da34c29ca646/1422328974467/Reactions+to+change+in+marital+status+2002.pdf.

The Final 40%: the way we think

Gilbert, Daniel. *Stumbling on Happiness*. New York: Vintage, 2007.

Kumar, Amit, Matthew A. Killingsworth, and Thomas Gilovich. "Waiting for Merlot: Anticipatory Consumption of Experiential and Material Purchases." *Psychological Science*, vol. 25,

10 (2014):1924–1931. https://journals.sagepub.com/doi/pdf/10.1177/0956797614546556.

Howell, Ryan T. and Graham Hill. "The mediators of experiential purchases: Determining the impact of psychological needs satisfaction and social comparison." *The Journal of Positive Psychology*, vol. 4, 6 (2009): 511–522. https://www.tandfonline.com/doi/full/10.1080/17439760903270993.

Jose, Paul E., Bee T. Lim, and Fred B. Bryant. "Does savoring increase happiness? A daily diary study." *The Journal of Positive Psychology*, vol. 7, 3 (2012): 176–187. https://www.tandfonline.com/doi/abs/10.1080/17439760.2012.671345.

Lyubomirsky, Sonja, Lorie Sousa, and Rene Dickerhoof. (2006). "The costs and benefits of writing, talking, and thinking about life's triumphs and defeats." *Journal of Personality and Social Psychology*, vol. 90, no. 4 (2006): 692. http://sonjalyubomirsky.com/wp-content/themes/sonjalyubomirsky/papers/LSD2006.pdf.

Koo, Minkyung, Sara B. Algoe, Timothy D. Wilson, and Daniel T. Gilbert. "It's a wonderful life: Mentally subtracting positive events improves people's affective states, contrary to their affective forecasts." *Journal of Personality and Social Psychology*, vol. 95, no. 5 (2008): 1217–1224. https://doi.org/10.1037/a0013316.

Emmons, Robert A., and Michael E. McCullough. "Counting blessings versus burdens: An experimental investigation of gratitude and subjective well-being in daily life." *Journal of Personality and Social Psychology*, vol. 84, no. 2 (2003): 377. https://greatergood.berkeley.edu/pdfs/GratitudePDFs/6Emmons-BlessingsBurdens.pdf.

Seligman, Martin E.P., Tracy A. Steen, and Christopher Peterson. "Positive Psychology Progress: Empirical Validation of Interventions." *American Psychologist*, 60, 5 (2005): 410–21. https://doi.org/10.1037/0003-066X.60.5.410.

Morewedge, Carey K., Daniel T.Gilbert, Kristian Ove R. Myrseth, Karim S. Kassam, Timothy D. Wilson. "Consuming experience: Why affective forecasters overestimate comparative value. Journal of Experimental Social Psychology." *Journal of Experimental Social Psychology*, vol. 46, 6, 986–992 (2010). https://doi.org/10.1016/j.jesp.2010.07.010.

Nelson, Leif D., and Tom Meyvis. "Interrupted consumption: Adaptation and the disruption of hedonic experience." *Journal of Marketing Research*, 45, 6 (2008): 654–664. http://pages.stern.nyu.edu/~lnelson0/Nelson%20and%20Meyvis.pdf.

Chapter 5. Is happiness a fluffy metric?

West, Michael A., and Jeremy F. Dawson. "Employee engagement and NHS performance." The King's Fund, 2012. https://www.kingsfund.org.uk/sites/default/files/employee-engagement-nhs-performance-west-dawson-leadership-review2012-paper.pdf.

Chapter 6. Discovering Happiness

Interviews

Shambler, Gemma, and Chris Hyland. "The Birth of The Happiness Index with Gemma Shambler and Chris Hyland." *Happiness and Humans*, September 14, 2020. https://open.spotify.com/episode/4L2sYKB2rWRuiPj9Bpl68n?si=mxTvQz5uQAOL45XrF-_fSA.

Chapter 7. Scaling Happiness

Interviews

Latter, Tony, and Matt Stannard. "Founding & Growing The Happiness Index Globally with Tony Latter and Matt Stannard." *Happiness and Humans*, September 14, 2020. https://open.spotify.com/episode/0Kpd9BIk4WYgAra7VT2MsD?si=vdPfGAwwQGWZWLPwojYg2w.

Further reading
Scott, Kim. *Radical Candour: Be a Kickass Boss Without Losing Your Humanity*. New York: St. Martin's Press, 2017.

Chapter 8. Happiness Biology and Chemistry
Huber, Robert, Kalim Smith, Antonia Delago, Karin Isaksson, and Edward A. Kravitz. "Serotonin and aggressive motivation in crustaceans: Altering the decision to retreat." *PNAS*, 94, 11 (May 1997): 5939–5942. https://doi.org/10.1073/pnas.94.11.5939.

Jonz, Michael G., Ekaterini Riga, A. Joffre Mercier, and John W. Potter. "Effects of 5-HT (serotonin) on reproductive behaviour in Heterodera schachtii (Nematoda)." *Canadian Journal of Zoology* (September 2001). https://doi.org/10.1139/z01-135.

Gonçalves, Leonor. "Psychologist Jordan Peterson says lobsters help to explain why human hierarchies exist – do they?" *The Conversation*, January 24, 2018. https://theconversation.com/psychologist-jordan-peterson-says-lobsters-help-to-explain-why-human-hierarchies-exist-do-they-90489.

Raypole, Crystal. "How to Hack Your Hormones for a Better Mood." *healthline*, September 30, 2019. https://www.healthline.com/health/happy-hormone.

Dopamine
Julson, Erica. "10 Best Ways to Increase Dopamine Levels Naturally." *healthline*, May 10, 2018. https://www.healthline.com/nutrition/how-to-increase-dopamine.

Fernstrom, John D., and Madelyn H. Fernstrom. "Tyrosine, phenylalanine, and catecholamine synthesis and function in the brain." *J Nutr.*, 137, 6, suppl. 1, (2007): 1539S-1548S. https://pubmed.ncbi.nlm.nih.gov/17513421/.

"U.S. Department of Agriculture, Agricultural Research Service." FoodData Central, 2019. fdc.nal.usda.gov.

Krach, Sören, Frieder Paulus, Maren Bodden, and Tilo Kircher. "The rewarding nature of social interactions." *Fron-*

tiers in Behavioral Neuroscience, vol. 4, 22 (2010). https://www.frontiersin.org/article/10.3389/fnbeh.2010.00022.

Ayano, Getinet. "Dopamine: Receptors, Functions, Synthesis, Pathways, Locations and

Mental Disorders: Review of Literatures." *Journal of Mental Disorders and Treatment*, 2:2 (2016). https://www.hilarispublisher.com/open-access/dopamine-receptors-functions-synthesis-pathways-locations-andmental-disorders-review-of-literatures-2471-271X-1000120.pdf.

"Dopamine." *Wikipedia*, accessed October 21, 2020. https://en.wikipedia.org/wiki/Dopamine.

Serotonin

Wilson, Debra Rose. "6 Ways to Boost Serotonin Without Medication." *healthline,* April 22, 2019. https://www.healthline.com/health/how-to-increase-serotonin.

Wilson, Debra Rose. "6 Ways to Boost Serotonin Without Medication." *healthline,* August 19, 2020. https://www.healthline.com/health/mental-health/serotonin.

Richter, Amy. "7 Foods That Could Boost Your Serotonin: The Serotonin Diet." *healthline,* August 31, 2020. https://www.healthline.com/health/healthy-sleep/foods-that-could-boost-your-serotonin.

Jenkins, Trisha A., Jason C. D. Nguyen, Kate E. Polglaze, and Paul P. Bertrand. "Influence of Tryptophan and Serotonin on Mood and Cognition with a Possible Role of the Gut-Brain Axis." *Nutrients*, vol. 8, 1 (January 2016): 56. https://doi.org/10.3390/nu8010056.

Young, Simon N. "How to increase serotonin in the human brain without drugs." *Journal of Psychiatry and Neuroscience*, vol. 32, 6, (November 2007): 394–399. https://www.ncbi.nlm.nih.gov/pmc/articles/PMC2077351/.

"Serotonin." *Wikipedia*, accessed October 21, 2020. https://en.wikipedia.org/wiki/Serotonin.

Oxytocin

Santos-Longhurst, Adrienne. "Why Is Oxytocin Known as the 'Love Hormone'? And 11 Other FAQs." *healthline*, August 20, 2018. https://www.healthline.com/health/love-hormone.

Wudarczyk, Olga A et al. "Could intranasal oxytocin be used to enhance relationships? Research imperatives, clinical policy, and ethical considerations." Current opinion in psychiatry vol. 26,5 (2013): 474-484. https://doi:10.1097/YCO.0b013e3283642e10.

Neumann, Inga D. "Oxytocin: The Neuropeptide of Love Reveals Some of Its Secrets." *Cell Metobolism*, vol. 5,4 (April 2017): 231–233. https://doi.org/10.1016/j.cmet.2007.03.008.

Bick, Johann, Mary Dozier, Kristin Bernard, Robert Simons, and Damion Grasso. "Foster mother-infant bonding: associations between foster mothers' oxytocin production, electrophysiological brain activity, feelings of commitment, and caregiving quality." *Child Development*, vol. 84,3 (2013): 826–40. https://doi:10.1111/cdev.12008.

Olff, Miranda, Jessie L. Frijling, Laura D. Kubzansky, Bekh Bradley, Mark A. Ellenbogen, Christopher Cardoso, Jennifer A. Bartz, Jason R. Yee, and Mirjam van Zuiden. "The role of oxytocin in social bonding, stress regulation and mental health: An update on the moderating effects of context and interindividual differences." *Psychoneuroendocrinology*, vol. 38,9 (2013): 1883–94. https://doi:10.1016/j.psyneuen.2013.06.019.

"Oxytocin." *Wikipedia*, accessed October 21, 2020. https://en.wikipedia.org/wiki/Oxytocin.

Endorphins

Berry, Jennifer. "Endorphins: Effects and how to increase levels." *Medical News Today*, February 6, 2018. https://www.medicalnewstoday.com/articles/320839.

Dinas, P.C., Y. Koutedakis, and A.D. Flouris. "Effects of exercise and physical activity on depression." *Irish Journal of Medical Science*, 180 (2011): 319–325. https://doi.org/10.1007/s11845-010-0633-9.

Kumar, Shiv Basant, Rashmi Yadav, Raj Kumar Yadav, Madhuri Tolahunase, and Rima Dada. "Telomerase Activity and Cellular Aging Might Be Positively Modified by a Yoga-Based Lifestyle Intervention." *The Journal of Alternative and Complementary Medicine*, vol. 21, no. 6 (June 2015). https://doi.org/10.1089/acm.2014.0298.

Bosland, Paul W. "Hot stuff – do people living in hot climates like their food spicy hot or not?" *Temperature (Austin, Tex.)*, vol. 3, 1 (January 2016). 41–2. https://europepmc.org/article/med/27227093.

Magrone, Thea, Matteo Antonio Russo, and Emilio Jirillo. "Cocoa and Dark Chocolate Polyphenols: From Biology to Clinical Applications." *Frontiers in Immunology*, vol. 8 (2017): 677. https://doi.org/10.3389/fimmu.2017.00677.

University of Turku. "Social laughter releases endorphins in the brain." ScienceDaily. www.sciencedaily.com/releases/2017/06/170601124121.htm.

Dinas, P.C., Y. Koutedakis, and A.D. Flouris. "Effects of exercise and physical activity on depression." *Irish Journal of Medical Science*, 180 (2011): 319–325. https://doi.org/10.1007/s11845-010-0633-9.

Berry, Jennifer. "Endorphins: Effects and how to increase levels." *Medical News Today*, February 6, 2018. https://www.medicalnewstoday.com/articles/320839.

"Endorphins." *Wikipedia*, accessed October 21, 2020. https://en.wikipedia.org/wiki/Endorphins.

Chapter 9. Practical Tips

Much of the science that underpins these tips comes from previous chapters, but here are some bonus studies in case you really want to get to the bottom of things:

University of Turku. "Social laughter releases endorphins in the brain." *ScienceDaily*, June 1, 2017. https://www.sciencedaily.com/releases/2017/06/170601124121.htm.

Harrison, S.J., A.E. Tyrer, R. D. Levitan, X. Xu, S. Houle, A.A. Wilson, J.N. Nobrega, P.M. Rusjan, and J.H. Meyer. "Light therapy and serotonin transporter binding in the anterior cingulate and prefrontal cortex." Acta psychiatrica Scandinavica, vol. 132, 5 (2015): 379–388. https://doi.org/10.1111/acps.12424

Robertson, Sally. "Doctors urged to prescribe woodland walks for mental health problems." *News Medical*, June 10, 2019. https://www.news-medical.net/news/20190610/Doctors-urged-to-prescribe-woodland-walks-for-mental-health-problems.aspx.

Davis, D. M., and J. A. Hayes. "What are the benefits of mindfulness?" *Monitor on Psychology*, 43, 7 (July 2012). http://www.apa.org/monitor/2012/07-08/ce-corner.

Buckle, Jane. "Aromatherapy for Stress in Patients and Hospital Staff." *Alternative and Complementary Therapies*, vol. 21, 5 (October 2015): 210–213. http://doi.org/10.1089/act.2015.29016.jbu.

Sánchez-Vidaña, Dalinda Isabel, Shirley Pui-Ching Ngai, Wanjia He, Jason Ka-Wing Chow, Benson Wui-Man Lau, and Hector Wing-Hong Tsang. "The Effectiveness of Aromatherapy for Depressive Symptoms: A Systematic Review." *Evidence-based Complementary and Alternative Medicine*, vol. 2017 (2017). https://doi.org/10.1155/2017/5869315.

Lake, James. "Acupuncture in Mental Health Care: Preliminary findings call for larger studies and improved study designs." *Psychology Today*, January 2, 2018. https://www.psychologytoday.com/gb/blog/integrative-mental-health-care/201801/acupuncture-in-mental-health-care.

Ruysschaert, Nicole. "The Use of Hypnosis in Therapy to Increase Happiness." *The American Journal of Clinical Happiness*, 56, 3. (July 2014): 269–84. https://

doi.org/10.1080/00029157.2013.846845.

Dunbar, R.I.M. "Breaking Bread: the Functions of Social Eating, Adaptive Human Behavior and Physiology." *Adaptive Human Behavior and Physiology*, 3 (2017): 198–211. https://doi.org/10.1007/s40750-017-0061-4.

Yorks, Dayna M., Christopher A. Frothingham, and Mark D. Schuenke. "Effects of Group Fitness Classes on Stress and Quality of Life of Medical Students." *The Journal of the American Osteopathic Association*, vol. 117 (November 2017): e17–e25. https://doi.org/10.7556/jaoa.2017.140.

Dunbar, R.I.M., Ben Teasdale, Jackie Thompson, Felix Budelmann, Sophie Duncan, Evert van Emde Boas, and Laurie Maguire. "Emotional arousal when watching drama increases pain threshold and social bonding." *Royal Society Open Publishing*, vol. 3, 9 (September 2016). https://doi.org/10.1098/rsos.160288.

Davis, Nicola. "Watching sad films boosts endorphin levels in your brain, psychologists say." *Guardian*, September 21, 2016. https://www.theguardian.com/science/2016/sep/21/watching-a-sad-films-boosts-endorphin-levels-in-your-brain-psychologists-say.

Chapter 10. Happiness at Work: Contemporary Philosophy and Evidence

Interviews

Stewart, Henry. "Employee Happiness in the UK with Henry Stewart." *Happiness and Humans*, August 9, 2020. https://open.spotify.com/episode/1sPcS24NkSVQZX7a1CRLsb?si=kCS-xep2QXW-EHisD2ivqg.

Nayak, Raj. "Employee Happiness in India by Raj Nayak." *Happiness and Humans*, August 11, 2020. https://open.spotify.com/episode/4PhE43KB9UdgD7Bts89Ze9?si=7GzM7VnuTK69-r0VHlbtOg.

Pau, Louisa. "Happiness in the Boardroom with Louisa Pau." *Happiness and Humans*, July 29, 2020. https://

open.spotify.com/episode/0qLVt41GpP1WeExUwtDOpL? si=ZbACNNoER2WIsTmEJzp8Bw.

Wallace, Natasha. "Happiness and Conscious Leadership with Natasha Wallace." *Happiness and* Humans, August 6, 2020. https://open.spotify.com/ episode/757GBC5W7D0pOT82mpWFsM?si=D--1VCdiSH-SisnyDQMC-w.

Windross, Norris 'Da Boss'. "Can music make you happy? with Norris 'Da Boss' Windross." *Happiness and Humans*, August 13, 2020. https://open.spotify.com/ episode/1MGVsCP2ffzmCtH3IWQ7u0?si=XCb7x6l9SvGbBP3tt-IXWw.

James, Brandon. "Happiness and Brand Marketing with Brandon James." *Happiness and* Humans, September 11, 2020. https://open.spotify.com/episode/7AYOj0DdBllnrSSViXmatA? si=IbVNufNMSBiggG0ERMcaCA.

Further reading and sources

Bellstrom, Kristen, and Emma Hinchliffe. "Reports of a Toxic Culture at Away and Misunderstanding Inclusivity." *Fortune*, December 6, 2019. https://fortune.com/2019/12/06/away-culture-slack-inclusivity/.

Bidault, Francis and Alessio Castello. "Why Too Much Trust Is Death to Innovation." *MIT Sloan Management Review*, 51, 4 (June 2010): 33–38. https://www.researchgate.net/ publication/290024720_Why_Too_Much_Trust_Is_ Death_to_Innovation.

Duhigg, Charles. "What Google Learned From Its Quest to Build the Perfect Team." *New York Times*, February 25, 2016. https:// www.nytimes.com/2016/02/28/magazine/what-google-learned-from-its-quest-to-build-the-perfect-team.html.

Porter, Kevin T. "Ellen DeGeneres turned kindness into a brand. Now the brand may bring her down." *Washington Post*, August 5, 2020. https://www.washingtonpost.com/

opinions/2020/08/05/ellen-degeneres-turned-kindness-into-brand-now-brand-may-bring-her-down/.

Wallace, Natasha. *The Conscious Effect: 50 Lessons in Organizational and Leadership Wellbeing.* London: LID Publishing, 2019.

Chapter 11. Employee Happiness: Research and Evidence

Interviews

Dawson, Jeremy. "Employee Happiness, Infection Rates & Patient Mortality within the NHS with Professor Jeremy Dawson." *Happiness and Humans*, September 8, 2020. https://open.spotify.com/episode/7AsNISmBsYzIGHUKgkPmkb?si=c2BYNZmBTeusHqw49ricOg.

Edmans, Alex. "Data and Research into Workplace Happiness with Professor Alex Edmans." *Happiness and Humans*, August 3, 2020. https://open.spotify.com/episode/5jodR4lNZP7Ny38kGvR5g2?si=xeZyEgdiTUa6VDGw6fztDA.

Giurge, Laura. "Employee Happiness Research & Employee Burnout with Laura Giurge." *Happiness and Humans*, October 12, 2020. https://open.spotify.com/episode/2DF8DiM2ddMHGjfFEhuMDT?si=BivVkuE2SNaKoIlnAnZXQA.

Happiness at work

Fisher, Cynthia D. "Happiness at Work." *International Journal of Management Reviews*, vol 12, 4 (December 2010): 384–412. https://doi.org/10.1111/j.1468-2370.2009.00270.x.

Happiness and performance

Bellet, Clement, Jan-Emmanuel De Neve, and George Ward. "Does Employee Happiness have an Impact on Productivity?" *Saïd Business School WP 2019-13* (October 2019). http://dx.doi.org/10.2139/ssrn.3470734.

Happiness and employee burnout

https://www.octanner.com/uk/global-culture-report.html

Laura Giurge's research is yet to be published, at time of writing, so watch this space!

Culture and brand are the same thing

Chamberlain, Andrew and Daniel Zhao. "The Key to Happy Customers? Happy Employees." *Harvard Business Review*, August 19, 2019. https://hbr.org/2019/08/the-key-to-happy-customers-happy-employees.

Happiness and profit

Alex Edmans, accessed October 21, 2020. https://alexedmans.com.

Edmans, Alex. *Grow the Pie: How Great Companies Deliver Both Purpose and Profit*. Cambridge: Cambridge University Press, 2020.

Happiness and the bigger picture

Hatfield, Elaine, Cacioppo Hatfield, John T. Cacioppo, Richard L. Rapson. *Emotional Contagion*. Cambridge: Cambridge University Press, 1994.

Kelly, Janice, and Sigal Barsade. "Mood and Emotions in Small Groups and Works Teams." Organizational Behavior and Human Decision Processes, 86, 1 (2001): 99–130. https://www.researchgate.net/publication/222829420_Mood_and_Emotions_in_Small_Groups_and_Work_Teams.

Ramarajan, Lakshmi, Sigal G. Barsade, and Orah R. Burack. "The influence of organizational respect on emotional exhaustion in the human services." *The Journal of Positive Psychology*, 3, 1 (2008): 4–18. http://dx.doi.org/10.1080/17439760701750980.

Barsade, Sigal G., Constantinos G.V. Coutifaris, and Julianna Pillemer. "Emotional contagion in organizational life." *Re-*

search in Organizational Behavior, 38 (2018): 137–151. https://
faculty.wharton.upenn.edu/wp-content/uploads/2018/12/
Barsade_Coutifaris_Pillemer-Emotional-contagion-in-
organizational-life.pdf.

Want to study at Yale for free?

"The Science of Well-Being." Coursea, offered by Yale. https://
www.coursera.org/learn/the-science-of-well-being.

Further reading

"No evidence that public have 'had enough of experts', study
finds." The University of Sheffield, June 3, 2019. https://
www.sheffield.ac.uk/news/nr/no-evidence-public-have-had-
enough-of-experts-1.846832.

Chapter 12. Happiness: Practitioners and Evidence

Interviews

Lim, Jenn. "Delivering Happiness and Employee
Happiness in the USA with Jenn Lim." *Happiness and Humans*, August 30, 2020. https://
open.spotify.com/episode/6fig58nojWNczXR1JD4Szp?
si=RRORh5AzQ8Sb3rXjwuHv3Q.

Rydahl, Marlene. "The link between happiness, performance and innovation with Malene Rydahl."
Happiness and Humans, August 31, 2020. https://
open.spotify.com/episode/1FwZiTZbT4P6VCPI5dx3Cg?
si=IB449tLDRcyzwjkiGuKWMw.

Bentzen, Arlette. "Employee Happiness & ARBEJDS-
GLÆDE with Arlette Bentzen." *Happiness and Humans*, Auust 13, 2020. https://open.spotify.com/
episode/32PVfWjSZY13h9MWiAamPC?
si=DmCQV1KUThOSV9KP_RWf9Q.

Fitzgerald, John. "Career Happiness with John Fitzgerald."
Happiness and Humans, September 29, 2020. https://
open.spotify.com/episode/3nNY9n5k16ptnn0bCraiyv?

si=D6iYVujJQhuNs1JSnVND-A.

Withane, Kevin. "Diversity, inclusion and the pursuit of happiness with Kevin Withane." *Happiness and Humans*, September 4, 2020. https://open.spotify.com/episode/3IpxiMF8rLRFqIOwB6x4bV?si=zqDzgaGESB2NB6Z6DBD2gA.

Slattery, Margot. "Linking LGBT, D&I and Happiness with Margot Slattery." *Happiness and Humans*, September 7, 2020. https://open.spotify.com/episode/62vUBJiN2tO2LCOXSzuMQS?si=CeubGEzLTxCkv2ln5MqfXw.

Pearcey, Nicola. "Happiness, Leading, Curiosity and Storytelling with Nicola Pearcey." *Happiness and Humans*, September 2, 2020. https://open.spotify.com/episode/4Eus07vnL4rljVT6PnLKYG?si=fjDuxjpzQsC0oE4-0YuQmg.

Lawrence, Louise. "Is Happiness a legal right with Louise Lawrence." *Happiness and Humans*, September 24, 2020. https://open.spotify.com/episode/2MRJLqIS7k6oMrKwrL8Wxb?si=HGxL8zGwSB-UjdHAUV9kzQ.

Jayne, Tabitha. "Nature, Biophilia and Happiness with Tabitha Jayne." *Happiness and Humans*, October 5, 2020. https://open.spotify.com/episode/3LU9Ed2QUVPKwQJyFE19Bd?si=x2UBXcjTSni3SsemIHV4Cw.

The importance of happiness at work

Buhr, Sarah. "Uber accused of wage stealing in new lawsuit from New York drivers." *TechCrunch*, June 2, 2016. https://techcrunch.com/2016/06/02/uber-accused-of-wage-stealing-in-new-lawsuit-from-new-york-drivers/.

Palus, Shannon. "The Tyranny of Customer Service Jobs." *Slate*, January 15, 2020. https://slate.com/human-interest/2020/01/away-suitcase-scandal-tyranny-of-customer-service.html.

Happiness and education
Rydahl, Malene. *Happy as a Dane: 10 Secrets of the Happiest People in the World*. New York: W.W. Norton & Company, 2017.

Happiness and performance
"Guide: Understand team effectiveness." *re: Work*, accessed October 21, 2020. https://rework.withgoogle.com/print/guides/5721312655835136/.

Duhigg, Charles. "What Google Learned From Its Quest to Build the Perfect Team." *New York Times*, February 25, 2016. https://www.nytimes.com/2016/02/28/magazine/what-google-learned-from-its-quest-to-build-the-perfect-team.html.

"How Do You Create Psychological Safety at Work?: Interview with Amy Edmondson." myHRfuture, July 14, 2020. https://www.youtube.com/watch?v=U_35pAviSnI.

Edmondson, Amy. "Psychological Safety and Learning Behavior in Work Teams." *Administrative Science Quarterly*, vol. 44, no. 2 (June 1999), 350–383. http://www.jstor.org/stable/2666999.

Happiness and progress
Amabile, Teresa and Steven Kramer. "The Progress Principle: Using Small Wins to Ignite Joy, Engagement, and Creativity at Work." *Harvard Business Review*, May 2011. https://hbr.org/2011/05/the-power-of-small-wins.

Happiness and diversity and inclusion
Dixon-Fyle, Sundiatu, Kevin Dolan, Vivian Hunt, and Sara Prince. "Diversity wins: How inclusion matters." McKinsey & Company, May 19, 2020. https://www.mckinsey.com/featured-insights/diversity-and-inclusion/diversity-wins-how-inclusion-matters.

Happiness and nature
Lowry, Christopher, J.H. Hollis, A. de Vries, B. Pan, L.R. Brunet, J.R.F. Hunt, J.F.R. Paton, E. van Kampen,a D.M. Knight, A.K.

Evans,a G.A.W. Rook, and S.L. Lightman. "Identification of an Immune-Responsive Mesolimbocortical Serotonergic System: Potential Role in Regulation of Emotional Behavior." *Neuroscience*, 146, 2 (March 2007): 756–772. https://doi.org/10.1016/j.neuroscience.2007.01.067.

Grant, Bonnie L. "Antidepressant Microbes In Soil: How Dirt Makes You Happy." *Gardening Know How*, accessed October 21, 2020. https://www.gardeningknowhow.com/garden-how-to/soil-fertilizers/antidepressant-microbes-soil.htm.

Glausiusz, Josie. "Is Dirt the New Prozac?" *Discover Magazine*, July 2007. https://discovermagazine.com/2007/jul/raw-data-is-dirt-the-new-prozac.

Chapter 13. The Happiness Index Data

The Happiness Index, accessed October 21, 2020. https://thehappinessindex.com.

Chapter 14. Happiness Across the Globe

Interviews

Ortlieb, Pamela Teutsch, and Rodrigo Rojas. "Employee Happiness In South America by Pamela Teutsch Ortlieb & Rodrigo Rojas (Partially in Spanish)." *Happiness and Humans*, September 16, 2020. https://open.spotify.com/episode/3wztlbPt0g6bQG6kjlRw1t?si=GeysZjiTkuL0bwa8UiDnA.

Wiking, Meik. "Happiness and Hygge across the globe with Meik Wiking." *Happiness and Humans*, October 23, 2020. https://open.spotify.com/episode/2WwWLiyEhbk2rI7LjDSKEd.

The Danes and happiness

Wiking, Meik. *The Little Book of Hygge: The Danish Way to Live Well*. London: Penguin, 2016.

The Dutch and happiness

Bloom, Laura Begley. "Ranked: The 20 Happiest Countries In

The World." *Forbes*, March 20, 2020. https://www.forbes.com/sites/laurabegleybloom/2020/03/20/ranked-20-happiest-countries-2020/#4db10fa87850.

Child Well-being in Rich Countries: A comparative overview. UNICEF Office of Research, April 2013. https://www.unicef-irc.org/publications/pdf/rc11_eng.pdf.

Happiness in the USA

Vultaggio, Maria. "U.S. Employees Are The Happiest." *Statista*, December 10, 2019. https://www.statista.com/chart/20223/employees-happy-us-world/.

Happiness in Southern Africa

Tutu, Desmond. *No Future Without Forgiveness: A Personal Overview of South Africa's Truth and Reconciliation Commission.* New York: Random House, 1999.

Mandela, Nelson. "Nelson Mandela talking about Ubuntu." Interview. https://www.youtube.com/watch?v=l-RUPwl5edA.

The Japanese and happiness

"Moai—This Tradition is Why Okinawan People Live Longer, Better." *Blue Zones*, accessed October 21, 2020. https://www.bluezones.com/2018/08/moai-this-tradition-is-why-okinawan-people-live-longer-better/.

Fukada, Shiho and Keith Bedford. "Tips for longevity from the oldest people on Earth." BBC, Worklife, January 10, 2020. https://www.bbc.com/worklife/article/20191218-tips-for-longevity-from-the-oldest-people-on-earth.

Airth, Johanna. "What the Japanese can teach us about super-ageing gracefully." BBC, Japan 2020, March 30, 2020. https://www.bbc.com/future/article/20200327-what-the-japanese-can-teach-about-super-ageing-gracefully.

Happiness in Australian cities

De Neve, Jan-Emmanuel and Christian Krekel. "Cities and Happiness: A Global Ranking and Analysis." *World Happiness Report*,

March 20, 2020. https://worldhappiness.report/ed/2020/cities-and-happiness-a-global-ranking-and-analysis/.

Happiness in Antarctica
Edwards, Monica and Laurie Abadie. "Clowning Around Lightens the Load: NASA Studies Team Dynamics in Antarctica." NASA, May 2, 2019. https://www.nasa.gov/feature/nasa-studies-team-dynamics-in-antarctica.

Happiness in the UK
"Surveys using our four personal well-being questions: A guide to what surveys include the four ONS personal well-being questions." Office for National Statistics, accessed October 30, 2020. https://www.ons.gov.uk/peoplepopulationandcommunity/wellbeing/methodologies/surveysusingthe4officefornationalstatisticspersonalwellbeing-questions.

Chapter 15. The Neuroscience of Happiness
Tyng, Chai M., Hafeez U. Amin, Mohamad N. M. Saad, and Aamir S. Malik. "The Influences of Emotion on Learning and Memory." *Frontiers in Psychology*, 8, 1454 (August 2017). https://doi.org/10.3389/fpsyg.2017.01454.

The Playbook. Boardwalk Pictures; Delirio Films; SpringHill Entertainment, 2020.

Chapter 16. Introducing the Quantum Way
The Happiness Index, accessed October 21, 2020. https://thehappinessindex.com.

Chapter 17. Freedom To Be Happy: The Business Case for Happiness
"Get happy! SFU researcher explores the power of positive giving." San Francisco University, accessed October 21, 2020. https://give.sfu.ca/stories/get-happy-sfu-researcher-explores-power-positive-giving.

Aknin, Lara. "Happiness, giving and The World Happiness report with Distinguished Associate Professor Lara Aknin." *Happiness and Humans*, October 30, 2020. https://open.spotify.com/episode/5h1VAczwUAJLz10fhJ80cc.

Aknin, Lara, J. Kiley Hamlin, and Elizabeth Dunn. "Giving Leads to Happiness in Young Children." *PloS one*, 7, 6 (June 2012). http://dx.doi.org/10.1371/journal.pone.0039211.

Hanniball, Katherine B., Lara B. Aknin, Kevin S. Douglas, and Jodi L. Viljoen. "Does helping promote well-being in at-risk youth and ex-offender samples?" Journal of Experimental Social Psychology, 82 (May 2019): 307–317. https://doi.org/10.1016/j.jesp.2018.11.001.

Further reading

Buettner, Dan, and Sam Skemp. "Blue Zones: Lessons From the World's Longest Lived." *American Journal of Lifestyle Medicine*, vol. 10, 5 7 (July 2016): 318–321. https://doi.org/10.1177/1559827616637066.

Claudel, Matthew, Emanuele Massaro, Paolo Santi, Fiona Murray, and Carlo Ratti. "An exploration of collaborative scientific production at MIT through spatial organization and institutional affiliation." *PloS one*, 12, 6 (June 2017). https://doi.org/10.1371/journal.pone.0179334.

Dizikes, Peter. "Proximity boosts collaboration on MIT campus." *MIT News*, July 9, 2017. https://news.mit.edu/2017/proximity-boosts-collaboration-mit-campus-0710.

Boosting ENPS: How to create loyal business advocates. The Happiness Index. https://thehappinessindex.com/wp-content/uploads/2019/05/Boosting-eNPS-Unicorn-1.pdf.

What really makes people happy at work? Insights from The Happiness Indicator – a real-time view of workplace happiness. The Happiness Index. https://storage.googleapis.com/stateless-thehappinessindex-co/2020/02/205682d9-inidicator-unicornv2.pdf.

"Why firms should treat their employees well." *The Economist*,

August 28, 2019. https://www.economist.com/graphic-detail/2019/08/28/why-firms-should-treat-their-employees-well.

ACKNOWLEDGEMENTS

As the author of this book I want to give a shout out and full credit to the team below for making this book happen.

Core Team
Researcher and Copy Master: Ellen Whitehead
Editor-in -Chief: Susan Furber
Data Scientist: Simas Janusas
Artwork and Design: Joe Wedgwood

Experts
Thank you to the following experts for taking their time out to be interviewed by me for this book. All the research interviews are live on The *Happiness and Humans* podcast. Louisa Pau, Alex Edmans, Natasha Wallace, Henry Stewart, Raj Nayak, Arlette Bentzen, Norris Da Boss Windross, Jenn Lim, Malene Rydahl, Gethin Nadin, Nicola Pearcey, Kevin Withane, Margot Slattery, Jeremy Dawson, Brandon James, Gemma Shambler, Chris Hyland, Tony Latter, Matt Stannard, Pamela Teutsch Ortlieb, Rodrigo Rojas Foncillas, Louise Lawrence, John Fitzgerald, Laura Giurge, Patrick Phelan, Roma Varma, Lara Aknin, Sarah White, Shreya Jha, Christopher Lowry, Serene Tan, and Meik Wiking.

Quokkas
A huge shout out to the people that made this book possible through your work at The Happiness Index. Adam Coleman, Alex Johnston, Jaqueline Barnett, Sasha Hanau, Caroline O'Keeffe, Chris Delaforce, Chris Caldwell , Chris Hyland, Gemma

Shambler, Hannah Patchett, Imogene Flynn, Jackie Dyal , Jim Brigden, Jodie O'Keeffe, Joe Wedgwood, Lucy Hennessy, Mark Thompson, Martin Colenutt, Matt Stannard, Neil Smyth, Clayde Snyman, Noelle Kelly, Pardis Samiee, Pat Phelan, Roma Varma, Rosanna Bull, Rosey Jarvis, Simas Janusas, Tim Stoller, and Tony Latter.

Sources
Respect to everyone mentioned in the references section. Without your work and dedication to this subject, this book would not exist. I am paranoid about missing people out of this section. If you spot anyone I have missed out, please DM me and I will add.

The Happiness and Humans Community
One final shout out to The Happiness and Humans Community for your continued work in striving for a more positive future. Join the community by following this link: https:// thehappinessindex.com/join-happiness-community/

ABOUT THE AUTHOR

Matt Phelan is a co-founder and Head of Global Happiness at The Happiness Index. In his day-to-day role, he is responsible for the global expansion of the business. Matt is the founder of The Happiness and Humans Community, host of the *Happiness and Humans* podcast, and author of *Freedom To Be Happy: The Business Case for Happiness.*

Printed in Great Britain
by Amazon